9-09

Ed Del Grande's House Call

ED DEL GRANDE'S
HOUSE CALL

Foolproof Tricks of the Trade

from a Master Contractor

Ed Del Grande

TV show host for
HGTVPro.com & DIY Network

VIKING STUDIO

VIKING STUDIO
Published by the Penguin Group
Penguin Group (USA) Inc., 375 Hudson Street,
New York, New York 10014, U.S.A.
Penguin Group (Canada), 90 Eglinton Avenue East, Suite 700,
Toronto Ontario, Canada M4P 2Y3
(a division of Pearson Penguin Canada Inc.)
Penguin Books Ltd, 80 Strand, London WC2R 0RL, England
Penguin Ireland, 25 St. Stephen's Green, Dublin 2, Ireland
(a division of Penguin Books Ltd)
Penguin Books Australia Ltd, 250 Camberwell Road, Camberwell,
Victoria 3124, Australia (a division of Pearson Australia Group Pty Ltd)
Penguin Books India Pvt Ltd, 11 Community Centre, Panchsheel Park, New Delhi – 110 017, India
Penguin Group (NZ), 67 Apollo Drive, Rosedale, North Shore 0745, Auckland,
New Zealand (a division of Pearson New Zealand Ltd)
Penguin Books (South Africa) (Pty) Ltd, 24 Sturdee Avenue,
Rosebank, Johannesburg 2196, South Africa

Penguin Books Ltd, Registered Offices: 80 Strand, London WC2R 0RL, England

First published in 2007 by Viking Penguin, a member of Penguin Group (USA) Inc.

1 2 3 4 5 6 7 8 9 10

Copyright © El Del Grande, 2007   All rights reserved

Illustrations by Suzanne Stephenson

This book makes every effort to present accurate and reliable information. It is not a substitute for professional electrical, plumbing, and other home building and repair service. If you are not completely confident in proceeding with any of the repairs outlined in this book, you should call a profes sional. Neither the author nor the publisher shall be liable or responsible for any loss or damage allegedly arising from any information or suggestion in this book.

ACKNOWLEDGMENTS

Who do you thank when you have everyone to thank?

In many cases when TV personalities get a book deal, it usually comes because their career is skyrocketing after just a year or so in "the business" and a publisher wants to get them in print right away. So when it comes time for them to write their acknowledgments, they can usually fit everybody's name on one page and mention all the deserving people in their lives who made their career and book possible.

In any case, the transformation from working as a laborer in a plumbing truck to landing a full-time career in the media business did not happen overnight. It has been a slow, steady process of family, friends, and work associates steering me in the right direction and offering me very good opportunities that helped me accomplish my distant goals. I wish I could list everyone who gave me a chance to prove myself over the last twenty years. But I'd need another book to do that. My thanks to all of you!

Goals are often very illusive; along the way I ran into many road-blocks, and sometimes things looked hopeless. But my mom told me when I was a kid that success comes from never giving up. If you keep trying long enough, something positive will eventually happen. All at once, good things did start to come my way. One amazing event led to another and before I knew it, I had the opportunity to write this book. Although when we first closed the publishing deal, my wife, Linda, and son, Brenton, jokingly pointed out to me that I had to read a book first before I could write one!

Well, I did write one, and I want to give special thanks to: Sue Stephenson for the illustrations, my friends at Kohler, HGTVPro, and Scripps Howard News Service. Our publishers: Lucia Watson (my wonderful editor), Maureen Sugden, Kate Stark, Lissa Brown, Molly Brouillette, Jessica Lee, Rebecca Behan, and Megan Newman at the Penguin Group. Our agents: Jay Mandel, Jackie Harris, Ken Slotnick, and Jeff Googel at the William Morris Agency. Thank you all for putting this book deal together. Also, for your enthusiasm for the project and, most important, for trusting me with the advance! One final acknowledgment to anyone that bought this book: THANKS!

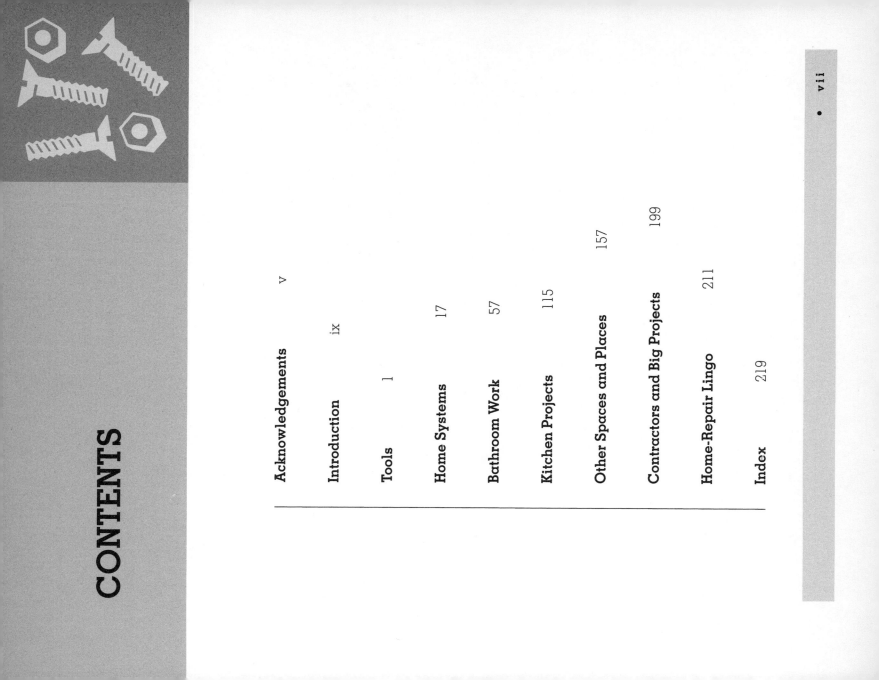

CONTENTS

Acknowledgements   v

Introduction   ix

Tools   1

Home Systems   17

Bathroom Work   57

Kitchen Projects   115

Other Spaces and Places   157

Contractors and Big Projects   199

Home-Repair Lingo   211

Index   219

INTRODUCTION

Home repair and remodeling have always been a part of my life. When he was young, the pipes called to my grandfather, and he moved from Italy to America to become a plumber. My father then joined the family business. I followed in their wet footsteps and was raised a plumbing prodigy. At five years old, I could name every control on a heating system, and although I did make several attempts in my early twenties to escape the construction field, I knew deep down that home repair and remodeling would be my destiny. In my late twenties, with three master contracting licenses under my belt, I took the plunge and started my own plumbing and contracting business.

The thing I liked about plumbing was that it involved every trade skill needed to build a house, and plumbers got to work with every contractor on the job, beginning with the excavation crews laying the water and sewer lines, all the way to the top, working with the roofers to run the vent pipes, and everything in between!

With all my experience working with so many contractors in so many different fields, I get a lot of special attention. In fact, whenever anyone finds out that I'm a master contractor in the home-improvement field, I become a marked man. The home-repair and bad-contractor questions and stories just start flying out and won't stop until I find a polite way to escape. I do like talking with people about home improvement, but there's a time and a place for everything. It happens to me at parties, sporting events, vacations, corporate meetings, restaurants, airports—it even happened in the green room of the *Today* show minutes before I was to go on air. Most people are so desperate for some good, solid advice from a real contractor that they forget that a public restroom may not be the best place to talk about their asphalt cracks. It's not something I consider to be a problem, but it does sidetrack me often enough to make me realize that just about every homeowner out there needs some extra help.

That's why I decided it was time to write a book about home improvement from a licensed master contractor's point of view. Some good home-improvement books have been written by people who may know the technical side of home repair and remodeling, but they may never have experienced life as a real working contractor. Trust me, there's a big difference between talking about how to do a home-repair job and actually doing it in the real world. On paper everything will go according to plan. I wanted to write a book that finally tells it like it is.

There is no magic bullet when it comes to good home repair. As much as physical skill is involved, there is also a mental process of handling stress, knowing when to change direction, and challenging yourself to come up with some pretty creative solutions. This book is for any handy homeowner who wants a behind-the-scenes peek at how a contractor tackles home-repair and remodeling jobs and what we really do when you're not looking. Let's get started with Ed's Essentials.

GET TO KNOW YOUR HOME LIKE YOU
GET TO KNOW A FRIEND

Just like your automobile, your home is a collection of moving parts and systems. Even though most people don't realize it, we all live inside a machine. In a sense, it is almost alive. In this way every home has a unique personality.

So don't let your home be a stranger; get to know it! Trust me on this. I have had the pleasure of working in countless homes over the past few decades, and the number-one reason I was able to provide accurate, quality service to all my customers was that I took the time to communicate with each home.

No, I'm not recommending that you talk to your home or listen for voices. Although I must admit that on very stressful jobs I've found myself begging and pleading water lines to "please stop leaking" after I tried everything in the book to repair them. Sometimes they do listen!

Anyway, I digress. What I'm talking about is knowing and understanding all the systems in your home and how they should work, then listening and watching for clues that will tell you that something may be wrong or where a problem could be. Your home communicates to you through the sights and sounds of its normal, day-to-day operations. And it's your job to know how to listen.

So along with teaching you home repair and remodeling with this book, I also want to educate you on how systems in your home work— that is, how one event can trigger a slew of other events. For instance, ever wonder how simply turning up your thermostat results in your house becoming warmer? Raising the thermostat is like knocking over the first domino in a long line of dominoes. One event leads to another, and if you know how your system should work, problems will be easier to pinpoint and repair.

For instance, in most cases, a heating thermostat is simply a small automatic switch that turns on your furnace controls, and in turn starts up your furnace. If you raise the thermostat and nothing happens at the furnace, there may be a chance that the main electrical power switch to the furnace is off.

Most codes require a furnace to have a remote "on/off" red electrical box switch outside of the boiler room so you can shut down the furnace or boiler from a safe distance in case of an emergency.

I've lost count of the number of service calls I've gone on, only to find that the remote emergency power switch had accidentally been turned off. I felt guilty, but I had to bill the customer a service charge just for turning on a switch!

So if you turn up the thermostat and nothing happens, the first logical step before calling a licensed technician should be to check if the electrical power switch to the furnace is on.

This is how you start to learn about pinpointing problems and saving on unnecessary service calls.

WORK WITH YOUR HEAD, NOT YOUR HANDS

Just as an athlete visualizes success before an event, a good do-it-yourselfer or professional contractor needs to do the same thing. As I've said, home repair and remodeling is mostly a mental game. Whenever I am about to tackle a job, I get a cup of coffee, look at the area I'm working in, and just think about every step of the upcoming project. I actually do the job in my head first, before I start. Not only does this relax me and put me in the right frame of mind, but it also triggers some red flags about what can sidetrack the job.

If you think about how the job will unfold, you'll know what could go wrong, and then you can be prepared. For example, if the first step in a job is to shut off the main water valve and you notice that your valve is in very poor condition, there's a chance it could break when you close it. You need to plan for that. If you just grabbed your tools without thinking and forcefully tried to shut off the old water valve and the valve broke, causing water to shoot everywhere, then you'd be in trouble. *Now* what do you do? How can you stop the water? Where are you going to get a new valve at this hour? Those are just a few of the questions that will rush through your mind as a heavy stream of water rushes through your basement. By contrast, if you'd previously visualized the possibility of a broken valve and then it did break, you'd have a backup plan to shut down the water and the materials on hand to re-place the valve.

It may sound funny, but you wouldn't believe the number of phone calls I've received from homeowners who've experienced the above scenario. And they had a stressful mess to deal with before they got to the actual repair.

As athletes play out a game in their mind before it begins, you need to think ahead. If you get in the "zone" *before* doing the job, not only will you confidently show up for the project with your A game, but you'll know enough to show up with extra tools and materials as well!

DO SOME HOMEWORK BEFORE
YOU DO SOME HOME WORK

Before you tackle any home-improvement job, study your project by getting all the information you can, along with getting a little hands-on experience. Information and execution go hand in hand to work like a pro. Even seasoned contractors read all the information they can about a new product they're installing. Most will also meet with a factory representative or another contractor first to get some hands-on experience with the product.

If I notice a helper on one of my jobs opening up a box and looking puzzled at the instruction sheet while sifting through parts, I know that trouble is brewing. I step in as soon as possible and get that helper off the job until I can walk him or her through the instructions.

You may be saying to yourself, "That's great, Ed, if you work for someone who can teach you, but how do you learn about the job if you're alone working on your own home?" Well, this brings us back to acquiring a little field experience first. Remember, field experience does not necessarily mean getting a job. Field experience can be volunteer time spent on a work site. It's usually pretty easy to land a volunteer job. No one I know turns down free labor!

There are a few different ways to volunteer your time, so find a way that fits your schedule and lifestyle the best. You can join a charity organization in your area that builds homes. I personally have worked on charity home builds for several projects, and trust me, this is bigtime home building! It's a real hammer-and-nails approach to home construction, and there are team leaders who will teach you step by step. You'll not only learn the trade, you'll also help deserving families get a home. It's a win-win situation.

If you're looking to learn a specific trade or skill, just about everyone has a brother-in-law, aunt, distant cousin, whoever, that's an employed tradesperson like a plumber or electrician. Many of these tradespeople work alone on the weekend to make a little extra money. Let them know you want to swap some weekend time for experience. If they realize that they can get some good help for just the overhead insurance costs and can waive paying you, it's great for everyone. They get the help, you get the experience.

Finally, find a friend, relative, or neighbor who's doing a home-improvement project similar to one you want to do. Act like a nice guy and tell the person you want to help. Do the job with that person and learn at his or her house! With your newfound experience, you can tackle your own job with confidence and even give the friend you helped a call to say it's time to maybe pay back the favor. This one is a little sneaky, but it works.

TIME TO LEAVE THE NEST

To sum it all up, these are my three *Ed's Essential Do-It-Yourself Rules*

Rule 1. Get to know your home like you get to know a friend.

Rule 2. Work with your head, not your hands.

Rule 3. Do some homework before you do some home work.

And always remember: A good sense of humor is the best tool in your belt.

Now that you have the confidence to go forward, follow me and I'll take you on a journey through the contractor's universe. Grab your hard hat and a coffee and let's go make a *House Call!*

Ed Del Grande's House Call

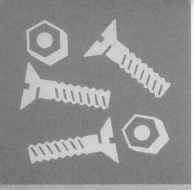

TOOLS

BASIC TOOLBOX   3

SPECIALTY TOOLS   4

   General   5

   Plumbing   7

   Electrical   9

   Carpentry   9

   Tile   11

BUYING TOOLS   11

LOANING TOOLS   12

RENTING TOOLS   13

RESPECTING TOOLS   14

Ed's words of wisdom on tools: *"You are judged by your work but envied for your tools"*

Since you're reading this book, chances are you enjoy puttering around the house and are looking to bring your home-improvement skills up to a more serious level. If that's the case, I have some good news and some bad news for you.

The good news is that when friends and family figure out you're a hard-core home-improvement buff, every holiday or birthday gift you receive from now on is going to be some type of construction tool.

The bad news is . . . every holiday or birthday gift you receive from now on is going to be some type of construction tool.

Gift tools are great because they will usually be fancy, fun, luxury gadgets instead of standard meat-and-potatoes tools. But keep in mind that good tools are always "work tools."

Most professional contractors stick to buying quality, useful tools that can do the job and take punishment instead of getting the bells-and-whistles stuff. Have your friends and family pay for all the cool tools. You can spend your own money on practical, investment work tools and equipment that will add value to your toolbox and professionalism to your projects.

BASIC TOOLBOX

Naturally, you need to start off with the basic hand tools needed to build your toolbox. Depending on your skill level and budget, you can custom choose the hand tools that will fit your needs. Homeowner hand tools should include the following:

Clawhammer
Assorted screwdrivers (Phillips and flathead)
Pliers (needle-nose and regular)
Cutting pliers
Slip-joint pliers (large and small)
Measuring tape
Utility knife
Hacksaws (large and small)
Wire brush
Assorted open-end wrench set
Assorted socket-wrench set
Adjustable wrenches (large, medium, and small)
Hex-key wrench set
PVC/wood handsaw

I suggest you purchase a hand-tool kit that comes complete with everything you need to get started—including the toolbox itself.

Most tool distributors will have a wide variety of basic and advanced hand-tool kits to choose from. The tools and attachments with these kits are comprehensive, and since you're buying a complete kit, you get a lot of bang for your buck. Trust me!

When I started my business, I bought a quality contractor's hand-tool kit with over a hundred tools and attachments. That gave me a good, solid starting point without the hassle of buying hand tools one at a time or trying to figure out exactly what I needed.

SPECIALTY TOOLS

Once you have your basic hand-tool kit, you can start to add specialty tools and power tools to your lineup and begin to build your own custom tool arsenal! Be patient, because it does take a little time, and this is the same way most new builders acquire their tools.

Start with a solid foundation of tools, and when you need a specific tool to tackle a new building project or repair, then get that tool.

As you build your toolbox, don't try to guess what new tools you may be needing for the future—you could be wasting your money. There's nothing more frustrating than a beautiful, brand-new tool that just sits on the shelf collecting dust because you have no use for it.

But on the flip side, when you do start a project and you need to buy a specialty tool to complete the job, there's nothing more fun than pulling a new tool out of the box and putting it to work right away!

I've compiled a list of specialty tools beyond standard hand tools that you may want to add to your tool stock. I'll also tell you how the tool is used, what you should know about tool grades, the skill level you need to use the tool safely, and I'll give you tips on working with the tool.

Keep in mind that this is just a basic list of tools that will allow you, the home-repair enthusiast, to do almost any project around the house. You should always keep an eye out for new items and technology on the market that will work best for you.

Don't forget, when working with any tool, always use the necessary safety equipment for the job, such as protective glasses, dust mask, and gloves.

General

Chalk line: A really fun tool! When you need a long, straight line to mark things like sheets of plywood, just give the canister that holds the line a shake, stretch out the line like a fishing reel, give it a snap, and magically a perfect straight line appears! Very old-school and very easy to use. Let's hope laser technology never totally replaces this tool.

Drill/screwdriver: (Cordless) Perhaps the best all-around and most laborsaving tool I've ever owned in my life. Don't cheap out on this tool! Choose one of the higher-grade eighteen-volt models with the "hammer drill" option, along with an accessory drill-bit/driver kit, and you'll have one of the most versatile tools ever invented. Novice to expert, this is a must-have tool for anyone, and you'll most likely use it on any home-improvement project you take on.

Hole saws: A hole saw kit contains a special bit and a variety of hole cutters for making tight finish holes through materials like fiberglass shower stalls, laminate counters, or hardwood floors. They'll fit most any type of drill. However, if you're drilling a lot of holes, a corded electric drill will work best. Use caution when working with any hole saw, especially the larger sizes!

Jigsaw: (Cordless or with a cord) This is a very versatile saw used to make scrolling custom cuts for crafting or finish carpentry. Also, this saw can be used for a lot of rough work, such as cutting holes for sinks in countertops. Remember, the jigsaw will only be as good as the blade you choose for it. I recommend getting an all-around jigsaw-blade accessory package with a variety of specialized blades for cutting through many different materials.

Reciprocating saw: This tool is a an icon in the construction industry and another must-have tool that can be used in just about every aspect of construction, except finish work. With the right blade, you can cut through just about anything—and I mean anything! With all that power, you do need to be careful where you cut. Plumbing lines and wires need to be avoided.

Right angle drill: A great drill with a unique feature. The head of this drill is set up with a ninety-degree right angle so the drill can be used between wall studs and floor and ceiling joists. Also, since it drills downward on floor surfaces, you get plenty of leverage. Caution: Get a model to match your skill level. The heavy-duty professional models are very strong and can spin you around!

Sledgehammer: I'm including this heavy-duty hammer on the list because it's one of the most overlooked tools. You should get two of these, a smaller handheld and of course the long-handled "heavy hitter." You'll be surprised how often you'll use them once you have them! For example, if you live in a cold climate and have a snow, just grab some long wooden steaks and your trusty sledgehammer. You can use the sledgehammer to drive the steaks in the ground around your driveway to mark it for the snowplow person.

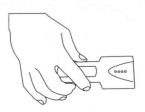

Stud finder: When they first came out many years ago, I was not a big fan of these tools. It always seemed that I could find the stud better than the "stud finder" did. But nowadays they make stud finders that are easy to operate and, more important, they're pretty accurate. Keep in mind my golden rule with studs: You'll never find a stud when you're looking for one, but you'll always find a stud whenever you're trying to avoid one! It even happens to the pros, so remember to be patient.

Torpedo level: This is a very accurate nine-inch-long, impact-resistant level that will fit in most toolboxes. Its bigger brothers, the two-foot and four-foot levels, can be inconvenient to carry around and hold when you work alone. Torpedo levels also have magnetic strips to attach to metal surfaces, and because they're so easy to handle, you'll find yourself using yours a lot.

Plumbing

Aluminum pipe wrenches: These are lightweight but heavy-duty wrenches with adjustable heads and very sharp teeth to grab onto pipes and fittings. A must for any serious plumbing work. Traditionally, pipe wrenches were heavy and bulky steel wrenches that really tired out your arms. The newer aluminum wrenches are very strong at just a fraction of the weight.

Basin cock wrench: If there ever were a specialized tool, this is it! Its main function in this world is to remove the faucet nuts located underneath a sink. Hence the name "basin cock" translates to "sink valve." If you need to change a faucet, you need one of these wrenches to work in tight spaces. It has a long center shaft with a hooklike gripping jaw on one end that swivels from side to side and a leverage arm on the other end to turn the wrench. Wear gloves— scrapes and bruises can be common when using this wrench!

Closet auger: This is the granddaddy of toilet tools. When a plunger just won't cut it and it's time to send in the big guns, grab your closet auger. This is a short, stocky, flexible steel snake about four feet long, with a crank handle on top. Be careful, because this tool is tricky to use and can easily scratch the bowl.

Cup plunger: This is the one tool that is most associated with plumbing. The rubber plunger end is wide open and shaped like a cup. Cup plungers run in sizes from small to large, and it's good to have a few different sizes on hand. The tool's main use is for lav sinks, tubs, and showers.

Drain auger: This is commonly called a hand snake, because it's a smaller, nonmotorized version of a power drain auger. A drain auger is handheld and turns with a manual crank. The coiled wire auger is spooled in a plastic or metal housing and is hand fed into small drain lines. Its main use is to clear small clogs in drain lines of the lav sink.

Force cup plunger: This is a heavy-duty-style cup plunger with a fold-out rubber extension funnel on the plunger end instead of an open cup. The extension funnel directs and forces the pressure deeper into large drain holes and creates a very good seal. Force cup plungers usually run in large sizes only. The main use is for toilets, but this tool also works well on utility fixtures with wider drain openings and kitchen sinks. Just don't use the toilet plunger in the sink!

Grabbing tool: This is one of my favorite tools! It's called by a few different names in different areas of the country, but there's no mistaking what this tool does: grabs objects in very narrow spaces such as a drain line or a garbage disposer. It's basically a small, flexible auger with a button that can be depressed on one end. When the button is pushed, four tiny metal fingers come out of the opposite end that can grab hair clogs and objects in most drains. Its main use is for lav sinks, shower stalls, and garbage disposers.

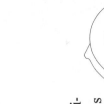

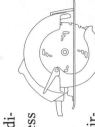

Propane torch: Self-lighting handheld model is best. You can use a torch for soldering copper pipe or whenever an intense heating flame is needed. Always have a fire extinguisher nearby when working with this tool and while we're at it, a fire extinguisher is an important tool-box accessory!

Tubing cutter: A cutting wheel scores and cuts the copper tubing as you spin it around the pipe while turning the pressure knob. You need to buy two types, the standard tubing cutter for working in open areas and a minicutter for pipes in tight spaces.

Electrical

AC current/voltage detector: (Contact type [A] or noncontact type [B]) A contact type is for bare wire ends while a noncontact-type current sensor detects current flow through shielded wires, wire nuts, conduit, and junction boxes. Keep in mind that checking for electrical power is just a basic test. When it comes time to do the actual electrical work, consult with a licensed electritian. Also, always follow the instructions for your type of electrical tester.

Wire strippers: Essential for working with any type of coated wires. Not only will this tool cut the wire, it will strip off the rubber coating to expose the bare wire for connections. Also great for RV and boat projects!

Carpentry

Circular saw: (Cordless or with a cord) A cordless version of the traditional corded electric circular saw does the job and, like most cordless tools, is easier to handle than corded models. A circular saw cuts studs, planks, and long sheets of plywood but is not as precise as a table or miter saw. Remember that a cordless circular saw is still a circular saw, so respect this tool and work carefully!

Combination square: When you are cutting wooden boards or planks, your cuts will be only as straight as your lines. The combination or "speed" square will give you straight ninety- or forty-five-degree angles by using a metal lip on the edge of the tool to line up with the edge of piece of wood itself, in order to "square off" the cut.

Power miter saw: If you get serious about finish carpentry, the miter saw will be your best friend. Note: A miter saw is not a "chop saw." A chop saw is generally used for cutting materials at ninety-degree angles only. A miter saw can cut at virtually any angle and swivel left to right and side to side. Its versatility is what makes it the perfect tool for cutting tricky angles.

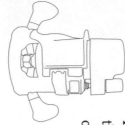

Router: (Cordless) When routers were available only in corded models, they were very intimidating to novices. Once the cordless models came out, they seemed more user-friendly. Now just about anyone can use this tool and get professional woodworking results. With the right router bits, you can do anything from creating moldings to trimming laminate counters.

Table saw: This is not a tool for the faint of heart, and I recommend getting some experience with this powerful device from an expert before attempting to work alone with one. It is a tool needed for cutting—or, as the pros say, "ripping"—planks and boards from end to end. Use every safety precaution available with this tool, no matter what your skill level!

Tile

Electric hammer drill: If your cordless drill does not have the "hammer" option and you need to drill through masonry materials, a hammer drill does the job. This tool rapidly hammers as it spins special masonry drill bits with built-in chipping heads. It quickly drills perfect holes through materials like tile, concrete, and cinder block. Corded models range from small, handheld novice drills all the way up to two-handled, heavy-duty professional models. Don't exceed your skill level; the bigger models are very powerful!

Tile cutter: Little cousin to the power wet saw. A tile cutter is a mechanical tool that uses a small cutting wheel on a slide arm to score the tile and then by pushing the handle down, snaps the tile to complete the cut. It works on the same principle as a glass cutter. Not as precise as the wet saw, but a whole lot cheaper to buy!

BUYING TOOLS

The preceding list represents just a fraction of the many specialty tools on the market today! I've used each one of the tools listed on a countless number of projects and have never been disappointed with any of my choices, because I always buy the best-quality tool I can possibly afford.

It is important to buy quality tools, even though they usually cost more, because once you get used to working with quality tools, your jobs will be less stressful. There's nothing more aggravating than not being able to work to your full potential because of a bad tool.

Remember that "best" doesn't mean "biggest." If you're a weekend warrior, you don't need to buy the expensive professional model. Many quality tool manufacturers make less powerful versions of tools for the part-time builder, keeping the quality intact but allowing you to save a little money.

The best strategy is to find a brand you like and stick with that company. Keeping all your tools the same brand will allow you to interchange accessories and add value to your collection by having a complete line of branded tools.

And again, remember to stay within your skill level when buying your tools. You may end up outgrowing a tool eventually, but not to worry—it just means that your skills are getting better, and you can always upgrade.

There's another advantage to buying high-end tools: If you do outgrow them, there will be a long line of people out there looking to buy them secondhand. That's not the case with cheap tools. Sometimes you can't even give them away!

LOANING TOOLS

I must warn you that once you've built up a pretty good tool investment, it's like winning the lottery. All your old friends, brothers-in-law, and work associates will start coming around to ask if they can borrow one of your tools. This seems harmless at first, but believe me, it can become a serious problem if you let people take advantage of your good nature!

If the borrower is someone you absolutely can't refuse, offer your services along with the tool. This way you can protect your tool from harm and get it back quickly.

If you start loaning out your tools with no strings attached, three things will eventually happen to your tools:

1. Every tool, blade, bit, and accessory you own will be damaged.

2. When an emergency comes up at your own home and you go to grab the tool you need, it won't be there, because someone else has it.

3. You'll be the one driving across town to retrieve a tool that you lent out, because the person who borrowed it is now too busy to return it.

When it comes to lending, the best offense is a good defense. If you really don't want to lend out your tools, then you must never ask other people if you can borrow one of their tools! That's the fairest solution.

However, there are some people in most towns who love to lend out their tools! In fact, they *exist* to share their tools with anyone looking to borrow one. These nice people are called "tool rental companies," and sooner or later you may find yourself having to rent a tool from them. Also, anyone looking to borrow your tools should be sent directly to these nice people as well!

RENTING TOOLS

Renting is a great option when you need a big, expensive tool that you'll use only once or twice in your life. For instance, a large jackhammer should be rented instead of purchased. Let's face it, how many times will most average people need to break up their concrete walkway?

But you do have to weigh your options when deciding if you should rent a tool. One disadvantage to renting any tool is that you are not making an investment in the tool. You pay the rental fee, you use the tool, and your money goes to the rental company instead of your toolbox. So first you have to decide if renting the tool will actually pay off for you in some way.

Depending on the tool, it can be very expensive to pay the money for a day's rent. You need to figure out how many work hours and also the wear and tear on your body the tool will save, compared to the cost of the day's rental fee for the tool. In effect, see what your time is worth! For instance, if you have to dig a two-foot ditch fifty feet long, you could save the cost of renting a power ditching tool by shoveling out the hole by hand. But if it took you all day to dig the hole, were eight hours of backbreaking work worth the cost of what renting the tool would be?

Worse yet, what if you hurt yourself digging and missed your full-time job on Monday? Now it's going to cost you money for *not* renting the tool! When I ran my business, I never missed a day of work due to injury. Outside of a little luck, the big reason I never got hurt was that I constantly tried to avoid putting myself in a position where I could get injured.

If I could rent a tool that would cut down my physical labor, I got the tool! Sometimes the extra costs would cut into my profit, but in the long run I made money because I never got hurt. Chances are you need to go to your job every day as well, so rent the big tools with no guilt when you feel they can help you with heavy work beyond your physical limits.

RESPECTING TOOLS

There's a limit to what mankind can do with eight fingers and two opposable thumbs. Think about it. As primitive as they were, stone tools are what brought man into the Stone Age. We have evolved into the society that we are today because of our modern tools. Take away today's tools and we're back in the caves. I don't want to get dramatic here, but most people take tools for granted, and I only want to point out the respect that tools deserve.

I love it when someone comes up to me with a very old tool that has been well cared for. As I look at the tool, the person will usually tell me it was his grandfather's favorite tool and now he gets to work with it and actually feel his grandfather's presence while working.

This is the point I'm trying to make: Your tools should be part of your life and legacy that you can pass on to others. It may sound crazy, but years from now, after you're gone, you'll still be able to have a presence in other people's lives through your tools. Tell me *now* what a tool is worth!

Once you understand the value of your tools, it's essential you maintain them on a regular basis. Cleaning and inspecting tools, especially power tools, is good not only for the tool itself, but also for your own safety.

I've lost count of the number of potential hazards I've spotted just from taking a power tool apart and inspecting it. Finding something wrong while cleaning one of your tools can be frustrating, but it's much safer to uncover a problem during cleaning than when you're using the tool while standing on a ladder.

Finally, respecting your tools will give you a healthy dose of caution and common sense when it comes time to work. If you're even a little hesitant about handling a powerful tool, you have no business working with that tool just yet. Take it one tool at a time, and let your skill and confidence grow along with the tools you acquire.

HOME SYSTEMS

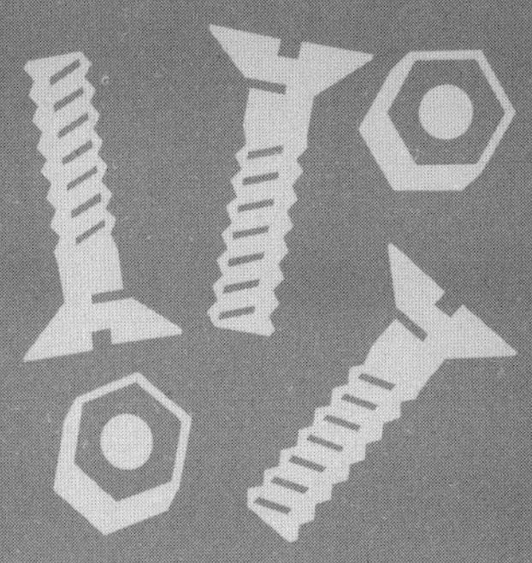

PLUMBING   20

Service plumbing and "a piece of the river"   21

Private versus public water   22

Home plumbing systems   24

The water system   25

Hot- and cold-water lines   27

Common types of water pipes   28

The drain system   29

The waste vent system   30

Common types of drains and vent lines   31

Plumbing system: final words   32

ELECTRICAL   33

Where home electricity begins   33

Circuit breakers and fuses   34

Service panel breakers 36

Circuit layouts 37

Electrical system grounding 38

Mapping your electrical system 39

Resetting a circuit breaker 41

Changing a fuse 42

Resetting GFCI outlets 44

Electrical wires 45

Electrical system: final words 46

HVAC 46

Energy and heat 47

Oil- and gas-burning systems 51

Water- and air-based systems 52

Choosing heating systems 55

HVAC systems: final words 56

Ed's words of wisdom on system maintenance: *"System maintenance is a constant battle. To win any war, basic training and regular inspections are vital."*

You have a lot more in common with your home than you may think. For instance, you both reside in the same neighborhood, you both depend on each other for support, and you both use systems that keep you running.

Even those systems are very much alike. Don't believe me? Well, take a look at the following comparisons:

A home has wires, you have nerves.

A home has water lines, you have veins.

A home has a furnace, you have a stomach.

A home has air conditioning, you have perspiration.

A home has sewer lines, you have . . . Okay, you get my point!

Like a human's systems, the systems in a home need constant attention. Just as most people visit their doctor at least once a year, you should check all your home's systems on a regular basis as well, so you can catch small problems before they develop into larger ones.

Along with making visual inspections, you need to learn the basics of how the three major systems in your home work: plumbing, electrical and heating, also known as HVAC. Otherwise, if you don't understand how something is supposed to operate, it's just about impossible to find a potential problem unless it's hitting you right in the face, like a big leak! By then it's usually too late and you're dealing with an emergency instead of a simple maintenance issue.

You may already be familiar with some of your home systems, but a refresher course always helps. And if you don't know how your home works, here's what happens behind the scenes:

PLUMBING

The plumbing system is by far the most serviced and most misunderstood system in your home. Because of that, we'll focus on plumbing a little more than on the other systems. Most people use their faucets or flush a toilet without even realizing the miracle that's just taken place before their very eyes. But in fact the invention of indoor plumbing was an amazing leap forward in history.

I'll never forget a poster I saw at one of our local building-supply houses when I started out in the construction business many years ago. It was a beautiful illustration of a plumber in a shirt and tie connecting a lead drain line, while an apprentice learning the trade looked on in wonder. The caption read THE PLUMBER, PROTECTOR OF OUR HEALTH.

This was decades ago, when indoor plumbing was new and people were thankful that such a system could actually be installed inside their homes. You may snicker a little nowadays at the image of a plumber wearing a suit and tie being compared to a doctor, but the fact is that the invention of indoor plumbing has stopped a countless number of diseases from spreading through our society. Just look at some of the unfortunate places around the world with no plumbing and you won't have to go far to imagine what your community would look like without clean water and sewers.

I don't want to go off track with all this, because my main goal is to educate you on how a plumbing system works so you'll have the knowledge and confidence to make some basic repairs at your own home. But along the way I also want you to realize how cool plumbing really is and what an engineering marvel your water and drain lines really are. Because when you understand this, you can acquire the focus and patience necessary to take on any plumbing project. So let's go, the pipes are calling!

Service Plumbing and "A Piece of the River"

The reservoirs, controls, pumps, and treatment components that public and private systems use to service your house with clean-water and wastewater lines are complicated. But you can sum up how service plumbing systems outside your home work with one familiar saying: Plumbing is the "circle of life." We take the water from the environment, use it, and return the water back to the environment.

How Public Water and Sewers Work: Public water starts at a place with a large fresh water source. The water is then cleaned, and an artifical river is created that flows into a city through a large pipe. Each resident draws from this flow of clean water for personal use, and then everyone drains their used water into a big waste river pipe. When the dirty water is diverted, filtered, and treated, it then flows back into the environment, and the circle is complete.

How Private Wells and Septic Systems Work: Private wells and septic systems can be created by drilling a deep hole into a naturally clean underground river, pumping up the springwater for personal use, then draining the waste water to a shallow tank to collect solids. As the dirty water is drained into the soil, through a leech field, the earth filters it on its way back down to rejoin the underground river, and once again the circle is complete.

Service Plumbing Summary: Believe it or not, that's basically how the water gets into your house and where it goes. We all use "a piece of the river" and then give it back. The amazing thing is that past, present, and future generations can end up using the same water over and over. Since no one's making new water, we all need to be extremely careful of what we put down our drain lines. If not, someday something may come back to haunt us, our family, and our community!

I've oversimplified how these utility systems work in order to give you a general understanding. Note that testing the quality and safety of any drinking water needs to be done on a regular basis, and you should follow all environmental codes and concerns when installing a sewer or septic system.

Now that you have some basic knowledge on how service plumbing works, let's move on to the subject of how your home's plumbing system works.

Private Versus Public Water

If you have a *private* well and septic system, it's pretty cut and dried where your plumbing system begins and ends. Usually a private system means just that: It's your private system. If it's yours, you own it, and the homeowner's responsibility begins at the bottom of the well deep in the ground and ends back in the ground at the septic system. This is a lot of extra financial and personal responsibility to have, and it can be costly to fix any problems that crop up. On the positive side, you won't get a water or sewer bill from your town!

If you have a private well and septic system, my advice is to find a licensed well and septic company to work with and get a regular maintenance schedule going for pumping out the septic tank and checking the well pump. Once you develop a good relationship with that company, it can also instruct you as to what you can do yourself to extend the life of your systems.

For instance, monthly treatments are available that you can easily add to the septic system yourself. The septic company can supply you with this septic additive and tell you how to do it and how often to add it. Similarly, the well person can set you up with your own test kits to check the water quality on a regular basis. These are just two examples of many things you can do, with the help of your service company, to protect your systems.

This way you're a part of your own maintenance crew, but in the event of a big emergency, like pump or drainage failure, you'll have a good relationship with your well and/or septic company. This usually means that all you'll need to do is call, and they'll get there quickly with repair equipment to have you up and running again!

Trust me on this. I have a private well and septic tank at my own home, and from the day I moved in, I started working with good well and septic companies and forged a strong relationship with them. Because I was loyal to them over the years, when the day came that I needed emergency help, they were there for me right away! It's a very helpless feeling watching waste water bubbling out of the ground in your backyard. That is *not* the time to grab the phone book and nervously start looking for someone who may not be able to help you until you next week!

If you have *public* water and sewers, I've got great news for you. It's not your responsibility to take care of your town's water and sewer system. However, as you already know, you will have to pay a water bill and a sewer tax so the city has the money to take care of the system for you. As they say, there's no such thing as a free lunch (or in this case a free flush!).

If you're on a municipal system, it can be a little confusing to understand exactly where your plumbing lines begin and end. Building codes vary, so you should contact your local utilities for the exact answer in your area. But in most cases the city's system ends at your curb valve and sewer tap on the town's main lines, located at the street. Usually, at the point the underground water and sewer lines enter your property, you are responsible for those lines and any maintenance needed for them, no matter where your water meter is located. However, many water utilities will service most meter problems.

The water meter is the control that the city uses to keep track of how much water you use. Depending on your area, some water meters are located at the street, many are located in the home, and a few are found somewhere in between. The water meter is typically the place where your home's main water shutoff valve is also located. FYI, your sewer tax is based on the gallons of water used and recorded on your water meter. It's assumed that if the water goes into your home, it also goes out of your home through the sewer system.

I bet the wheels are turning right now, and you may be thinking, "Hey, wait a minute, Ed! I fill a big swimming pool every year and water my grass, and that doesn't go down my sewer!" Good point, and if that's the case, you can call your water department to see if they approve having a second water meter installed and registered for an outside water line only. Many water boards okay this setup, and the water used for things like pools and lawns can be recorded on the remote meter and deducted from your sewer bill.

You're learning valuable contractor tips and tricks already, and we're not even in the house yet. Remember, even though public and private water and waste systems are completely different, once past the water meter or well tank, every home plumbing system works the exact same way inside.

HOME PLUMBING SYSTEMS

The term "indoor plumbing" has always meant something special to me. I've been involved with a large number of houses that I've seen transformed from an empty space into a beautiful place to live and raise a family. Hands down the most impressive thing that I see upon completion of all these jobs happens when I take the family into their brand-new bathroom and flush the toilet to show them it works. That never fails to bring a big smile to everyone's face!

The incredible thing is that as simple as it may seem, the action of flushing a toilet is the end result of everything we've just talked about. All of the system controls, valves, and piping work in perfect harmony to complete the goal of what a plumbing system is designed to do: get potable water into a house through the water lines, then get the nonpotable water out of the house through the drain lines.

"Potable" and "nonpotable" are very powerful terms in plumbing. They are used a lot in the construction industry but outside the industry those words don't come up very often. No one says, "Honey, get me a glass of potable water!" But we all use potable water every day of our lives and in the process create nonpotable water. Simply put, potable water is water suitable for drinking and bathing, nonpotable water is not.

So that's it. We all have just two types of water flowing through our houses: clean water and dirty water. That means we have only two types of plumbing water pipes in our houses: clean-water lines and dirty-water lines.

So far so good, but the tricky part comes in when you break down these two systems further. The clean-water lines split off into two separate potable hot- and cold-water systems, while the dirty-water lines split off into two separate nonpotable drainage and venting systems.

Just as water lines and drain lines carry completely different water through your home, I'm going to separate them into two different sections and break down each system for you step by step.

THE WATER SYSTEM

Every home usually has just one cold-water line entering through the foundation, or through the concrete slab if there is no basement or crawl space in the home. Your first job is to locate and become familiar with the area where the water main enters your home. If you live in a condominium, you should still have your own separate cold-water service line and main valve.

Once inside, the water line should connect to a *main water shutoff* valve just before the water meter. Even if your meter is located outside at the street, you should still have a main water valve where the line enters the house. If you have a private well, after the well water line enters the house, it will go directly to your well pressure tank. Then you should have a main water shutoff just after the pressure gauge on the tank feed line to your home.

A private *well pressure tank* is very easy to spot. It's a tall, thin water tank without any pipes coming out of the top. The well pump fills the tank from the bottom, and a rubber diaphragm with pressurized air on one side fills up like a balloon inside the tank and creates water pressure for your home. Basically, a well tank is not designed to hold water, but rather its main function is to store pressure for the water system. The more water your pump pushes into the pressure tank, the higher the water pressure will go! (Do not exceed 80 psi.)

Public water systems usually get their pressure from the town's water towers or storage tanks located at higher elevations. In this case gravity itself will supply the water pressure to your home. The lower you are relative to the water source or tower, the higher your water pressure should be. (Again, do not exceed 80 psi.)

Regardless of whether your water meter is in the house or at the street, or whether you have a well tank, the start of your indoor potable-water system begins inside at your home's main water shutoff valve.

If you don't know where your main water shut off valve is located, my first advice is to find it as soon as possible. To do this, you can check with the contractor who built your home, with the previous owner, or with the maintenance crew of your condo or apartment building. Once it's been located, you also need to ask about shutdown procedures for your type of main water shutoff valve.

When you have all this necessary information on the valve, I recommend that you close and open the valve to make sure it works. This way you will be familiar with the operation of the valve, which should allow you to keep a cool head during a water emergency. Also, don't keep this information to yourself. Everyone who lives in your home should know where the water main shutoff is located and how to use it.

A good idea is to get a big red tag and mark the valve EMERGENCY WATER SHUT OFF, along with closing instructions. This way it's easy to find and will remind everyone in the home how the valve is turned off.

Many homeowners don't consider looking for and tagging a main water valve to be a home-improvement project, so they never do this job. As a result, water damage often becomes much worse, because so many emergency leaks are never shut down in time!

Hot- and Cold-Water Lines

After the indoor main water shutoff valve, the residential hot- and cold-water systems begin. There the *main feed line* starts. This line supplies the water flow for things like sprinklers, as well as for both the hot and cold piping, so it is usually three-quarters to one inch in diameter before the line separates.

After it splits into hot and cold lines, the pipe usually reduces to a half inch in diameter to supply water to all the fixtures. This way both the hot- and cold-water systems have a good flow and equal pressure.

The split takes place at a tee fitting where the main line now goes in two directions. One side of the tee goes on to supply cold water to the house, while the other side feeds the water heater. At the water heater inlet connection should be a valve called the *hot water shutoff*. As the name says, this valve will close only the hot-water system.

The hot-water piping on the outlet side of the water heater is the start of the hot-water piping for the house. The hot- and cold-water lines are now two separate systems and will run in parallel throughout your house to supply any area needing water. These lines do not connect to each other again until they meet at the fixture itself.

That's it. Just about every hot and cold potable-water system is basically set up this same way. Remember, though, that there are a few different materials used for water lines, and the first thing you need to do is identify the type of piping your house has before you can attempt any plumbing repairs.

I'm going to describe the most common types of water piping found in today's houses. This way you can determine the kind of water pipe in your home and learn a little bit about how it should be handled. Detailed projects will come later, but for now you need to start off by knowing the material your water lines are made of and the characteristics of that particular pipe.

Common Types of Water Pipes

Copper pipe: Copper is by far the pipe material most found in today's homes. It has been around for decades and is a very reliable pipe for water systems. It is easily identified by its "copper" color and visible markings. Red lettering means standard "M" grade, and blue lettering is a heavy-duty "L" grade. The shine and color will dull with age, so clean up a spot to confirm that a pipe is copper. Installing and working with copper is a labor-intensive job, because most of the standard fittings used to join copper piping are soldered in place with a torch. Compression fittings can be used, but they also require work to tighten them into place with wrenches. Besides a complete soldering kit, a tubing cutter is a must-have tool to cut copper pipe properly.

CPVC pipe: Designed for potable-water systems, CPVC (chlorinated polyvinyl chloride) is the approved rigid plastic piping for hot- and cold-water lines in many areas (check your codes). Its cream color and clear markings usually make it easy to spot. CPVC was created to replace copper piping, but even though it's popular it never completely supplanted copper. Working with and joining CPVC is fairly easy and can be done with glue-in or compression CPVC fittings, and the pipes are easily cut with a CPVC cutter.

PEX pipe: This pipe has recently taken the industry by storm! PEX (polyethylene cross-linked) is very easy to work with, because it's extremely flexible and comes in very long coils. The color of this pipe can be semiclear gray, red, blue, or white and the kind of material is clearly marked. Entire lengths can be run from basements to attics, and specialty crimp on fittings make joining PEX pipe a snap when the need for a fitting is required. Pipes cut like butter with a PEX scissors cutter. No matter the color, all PEX piping is the same. But using different colors will help you identify the lines. For instance: hot water can be red and cold water blue.

Galvanized or brass pipe: This is really old-school stuff. Usually found in older homes, the battleship gray (galvanized) or dirty gold (brass) color is a dead giveaway that it's time to update your water lines! These pipes use threaded fittings and may require a threading die kit for repairs.

When you can identify the different types of water lines found in a home, it will give you the confidence you need to asses the condition of your water lines and deal with repairs on a more professional level. In most cases, if the existing water lines are in pretty good condition, you should make the repairs with the same type of piping and not try to "mix and match" water lines.

Also, if you're working with a plumber and know what kind of water pipe is in your home, it will make the job go easier. You can give the plumber your piping information over the phone, which may save some time and money, since the plumber can then plan and prepare the materials for the house call ahead of time.

The Drain System

Just as most homes have one main water line, there is also one main drain line. Septic system or sewer, once inside a home all gravity drains work the same way. The only variation on this would arise if for

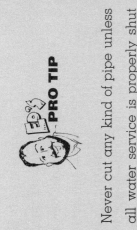

PRO TIP

Never cut any kind of pipe unless all water service is properly shut off and you are 100 percent sure of what type of line you're working with.

some reason—and it does happen—your home drain system ends up lower than the septic or sewer main drain line entering the home.

Obviously, if your inside waste pipe ends at a lower height than the waste line outside the house, the water will not flow uphill. In this case you need to have a piece of equipment installed called a *sewer ejector*. Basically, a sewer ejector is a closed pit sunk in the basement floor with a powerful pump that will collect the waste water and pump it up to the septic or sewer drain. Then gravity should take it from there!

Otherwise, gravity house drains all work the same way. The drain system starts with a very large main drain for the house, usually three to four inches in diameter. Think of this main drain line as a tree trunk, and off that main trunk smaller branches will go in different directions. In fact, these smaller drains are referred to as *branch lines* by many contractors.

Each fixture installed in the house will have its own smaller branch line to discharge its waste water into. The only exceptions are usually the toilet lines. Since more waste water flows through a toilet line, the drains will stay three to four inches in diameter. Drain lines travel through the entire house and will usually follow the water lines right to the fixtures.

Drain lines connect to a fixture with a U-shaped fitting called a *fixture trap*. Some fixtures have built-in traps, but most traps are located on the drain system itself. The big misconception many people have about fixture traps is that the traps are installed on drain systems to "trap" small objects from going down the drain. The actual purpose for a drain trap is to trap a plug of water so sewer gases from the system don't enter your home.

The drain system may end at the fixtures, but that is only half the story for your waste system. Drains go down, so there's no other place to go but up—and that's where your *waste vent* system takes over!

The Waste Vent System

When water flows down a drain line, a vacuum behind the water flow can form, creating a partial *air lock* and slowing down the water flow.

The air lock can also siphon the water plug from a trap, making gurgling sounds and allowing sewer odors to enter a home. One or both of these problems can spell bad news! Why doesn't this happen with most modern plumbing systems? Because of the waste vent system.

Try a simple experiment so you can see what air lock is and how vent pipes work. I'm sure you've done this experiment before but never thought of it in terms of your house's plumbing. Take a glass of milk and dip a clear straw into it. Place your finger over the top of the straw and raise the straw. You'll notice that the milk stays in the straw. Now lift your finger off the straw.

Congratulations! You've just created an air lock inside the straw, then vented the straw by raising your finger to break the vacuum, allowing the milk to flow freely. This is essentially the same thing that takes place in your vent system every time you flush a toilet or drain a sink, tub, or shower. And you thought those stinky pipes sticking out of your roof were just for show!

A vent line is installed with a tee fitting after a fixture trap and continues to run upward and may tie in to other vent lines before going through the roof. Some systems may not be vented, and we'll discuss those later.

Common Types of Drains and Vent Lines

PVC pipe: This white plastic pipe has changed the plumbing industry! PVC (polyvinyl chloride) is now the dominant type of pipe used for drain and vent lines. It's easy to handle and connect with primed and glued fittings. PVC is a rigid and rust-free pipe, and it also cuts easily with a wide, short PVC saw.

ABS pipe: The lost cousin to PVC. ABS (acrylonitrile butadiene styrene) is black plastic pipe and was very popular for a while because it usually costs less and is even easier to install than PVC! However, time showed that it was not as rigid as PVC, and it never succeeded in replacing PVC pipe.

Cast-iron pipe: This black, heavy iron pipe is what I learned to install as a kid, and all I can say is, "Thank the plumbing gods that PVC was invented!" However, cast iron is still used today because of its strength and water-noise suppression, but it can corrode over time. Today's cast iron connects with banded clamp couplings or rubber gaskets, and that sure beats the molten lead joints we had to pour years ago! This is a very heavy, labor-intensive pipe to work with, and snap cutting it can be a difficult job.

Copper drainpipe: Large, thin-walled copper pipes were once popular to install for drain-system piping. It's a gold-colored, sturdy metal pipe, which did work well for drain lines. The fittings were usually brass, soldered in place, and many of these copper drain systems still survive today! Chances are the only work you'll do with copper drains is repair projects. Installing copper drains is not cost-effective for any new construction.

Lead pipe: Old lead drain lines are easy to spot. Lead is a dull gray, soft, sloppy-looking pipe, and, unbelievably, some are still around. If you have problems with a lead drain (and you will), the best solution is to "get the lead out!" Don't try to repair lead pipes—replace them.

Plumbing System: Final Words

As you can see, your plumbing system is not just one system but many different systems working together in a long chain. Every link in this chain has to work to allow you the privilege of doing simple tasks like washing your hands with warm water or flushing the toilet.

When working with plumbing, you need to be patient and understand that frustration and plumbing go hand in hand. People constantly ask me, "How come I always keep getting leaks no matter what I do?" Well, the short answer is that you can never actually fix your plumbing system. At best, all you can do is contain the water in your pipes for a period of time. Water's job is to flow everywhere, and it will eventually find a way to flow out of your pipes. That's the nature of plumbing!

ELECTRICAL

Years ago, I was watching one of the late-night talk shows, and they had on a 102-year-old man who was in great physical shape and still sharp as a tack. This was a man who went from reading books by candlelight to speaking on a cell phone while surfing the Net, in one lifetime! He was one of the few people who had really "seen it all."

Since the man had had such a unique opportunity to have witnessed all the technology that came along in the last century, the host felt compelled to ask, "What has been the greatest invention you've seen?" You would think that this would be a hard question to answer and the man might have to ponder for a bit. But in fact he responded before the host even finished the question. "Without a doubt," he said, "getting electricity in my home was the greatest invention I've ever seen, and nothing else before or after that came close!"

As precious as electricity is to us all, never lose sight of the fact that behind all the bright lights there is a very dark side to electricity. For that reason I'm keeping the electrical sections of this book very simple and very basic. I want you to learn how your electrical system works but, more important, I want you to value your safety and always consult with a licensed electrician before starting *any* electrical project.

Where Home Electricity Begins

Utility-company service wires are attached to your home underground or aboveground at a safe height to a fitting called a *service head*, and then the service wires run down the side of the home through a protective sleeve into your *electric meter*. The electric meter measures how much electricity enters a home, and—as I'm sure you know—you're billed for that use. After the current passes through the meter, it goes into your home's *breaker* or *fuse box*, but many meters may have a *main power shutoff* outside.

You should locate your main power shutoff with an electrician and check out your box to ensure that you have a standard box setup. This will avoid any confusion when you need to service a breaker or fuse. The service wires from the electric meter should feed the breaker box with three wires: two main power or *hot* wires that are usually black or red and one main *neutral* wire that is usually white. Believe it or not, in most cases just these three wires are the main electrical connections for the entire house!

The white neutral wire connects to the *neutral bus bar*, while each one of the two main hot wires carry 120 volts and separately connect to the main power shutoff, usually at the top of your breaker box. Essentially, your home electrical system begins at the main power shutoff, which is located at your electric meter. Remember, this shutoff only stops the flow to your home's circuits—the utility electrical feed lines will still be live!

Any concerns you have with the electric meter, service wires, or service head, as well as system grounding issues, should be addressed by the utility company or a licensed electrician.

Circuit Breakers and Fuses

There are two basic types of electrical systems. The main power-shutoff switch for the system I described is usually found on newer or updated electrical systems using *circuit breaker* switches. As a matter of fact, the main switch itself should be a very large circuit breaker. However, some older homes may still be using *fuse*-type systems, and in that case you may have a *pullout block* in place of a switch.

Every box has a circuit panel with breakers or fuses located inside the service box. Breakers or fuses are like the security guards for your electrical system. Their job is not to supply electricity to your home but to protect your wires from overheating by thermally *tripping*, if it's a breaker, or *blowing*, if it's a fuse. Each has an amp rating for the maximum amount of current allowed to a circuit, and if the circuit gets overloaded or shorts out, breakers and fuses shut down the circuit. Never change the amp rating! AMP stands for amperage and that is one of the standard measurements of electrical current in a circuit.

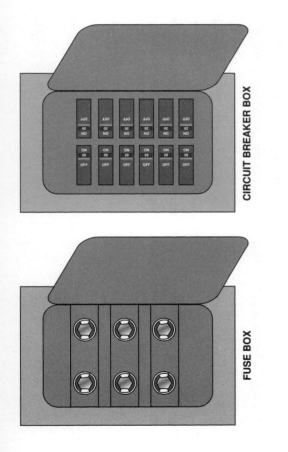

FUSE BOX

CIRCUIT BREAKER BOX

Finding out if your home has a breaker system or a fuse system is pretty easy once you locate your service box. If you open the box and see long rows of switches lined up like soldiers inside the box, that's a circuit-breaker system. If you see round circles in a line with clear tops that look sort of like glass eyes, that's the older-type fuse system.

Fuse systems are outdated compared to breakers. If a fuse burns out, it has to be discarded, and it can be annoying always having to have a new fuse of the correct ampage on hand to replace the blown one. Circuit breakers conveniently rely on thermal switches that trip like a mouse trap and can easily be reset.

If you have an old fuse system, I recommend hiring an electrician to update your system. It's a very wise and safe investment. Later in this chapter, I will explain how to replace blown fuses. That's the extent of what you should do to service older systems. But I'll focus primarily on the newer breaker *service panels* and how they work, since that's what's used in most homes.

Service Panel Breakers

Most main power shutoffs are located inside the breaker box at the top of the service panel. The main shutoff is usually a very large amp breaker switch and has two connections on the incoming side of the switch. Each one of the two 120-volt service wires connects to one of the two incoming terminals on the switch. On the outgoing side of the switch are two corresponding 120-volt bus bars. These 120-volt "hot" copper tracks supply power to all the other breakers in the panel. Voltage or volts is the measurement of electrical power flowing in a circuit.

Most of the circuit breakers in the panel may be 15- or 20-amp, 120-volt breakers plugged in to one of the two 120-volt bus bars. A few of the breakers may be 30-amp, 240-volt breakers that attach to both of the 120-volt bus bars. Get it? So 120 plus 120 will equal a 240-volt circuit breaker. The bigger breakers will power 240-volt heavy-duty equipment such as electric clothes dryers, ovens, or even water heaters.

Each breaker will protect its own electrical circuit and will be amp-rated by the installing electrician according to the potential draw on that circuit. You don't want to have a breaker underrated for a circuit, because that could lead to constant tripping of the breaker. On the more cautious side, you don't want to have a breaker overrated for a circuit, because that could lead to overheating of the circuit wires, causing a hazardous situation. Remember the Three Bears story: You want a breaker that's just right!

The most common cause for tripping a breaker is usually simply overloading an outlet. We've all used those adapters that can turn one outlet into four outlets, and even though it seems harmless, adding multiple outlets can change the proper layout of your circuit. It's very easy to overload a circuit by plugging in too many appliances. For instance, a normal toaster, refrigerator, and microwave on the same outlet box rated for 15 amps can easily cause an overload for that circuit breaker.

Another cause of tripping breakers is a *short circuit*. That can happen when bare wires come in contact with each other or metal objects, shorting the circuit. In the troubleshooting section, we'll get into more detail about overloads and shorts and how to properly reset circuit breakers.

Circuit Layouts

Every breaker in the panel has its own circuit that services a specific area in your home. A circuit is simply an electrical loop, leaving a breaker with a hot 120-volt wire that supplies power to fixtures or outlets. Then the circuit loops back to the panel box with a neutral wire into the neutral bus bar. Hot wires are usually black and neutral wires are usually white.

The number of appliances and outlets a circuit can have on its loop is calculated according to its potential draw of electricity. For instance, a circuit for just lights, switches, and outlets can have several lights and a few outlets all on one circuit, because the projected use may not be a heavy draw. Plus, if any switch is placed in the "off" position, it will *interrupt* a section of the circuit, reducing the load further by taking that light or outlet completely off the loop. Hence the saying "You're out of the loop!"

On the other hand, some circuits may have only one fixture on the entire circuit loop. Heavy-use kitchen appliances like garbage disposers and dishwashers may need their own dedicated circuit to be sized properly. These appliances are *hardwired*, which means that the electrical wires connect directly to the appliance, rather than plug into a wall outlet.

Microwave ovens in most cases plug in to an outlet and also have a heavy draw potential. In that case the microwave oven's outlet in the kitchen may be the only one on the entire circuit! The trick is planning ahead and studying the plans to properly lay out every circuit.

Most circuits will be 120 volts, but for the high-voltage equipment mentioned, like electrical dryers, these circuits will be high-voltage, 240-volt circuits for that one big appliance. A 240-volt circuit will double the circuit power by running two hot 120-volt feed lines from the 240-volt breaker, but it will still loop back to the panel with only one neutral return line.

Installing, sizing, and laying out electrical circuits is best left to licensed professional electricians. However, it's important you understand the basics of how circuits and breakers work. This way you can do simple maintenance and repair jobs to your own electrical system with confidence.

Electrical System Grounding

We've gone over the panel breakers and basic circuit information with black-and-white, two-wire circuits. Newer systems also have a third wire, a green one, for each circuit, called the *grounding wire*. Grounding adds additional protection against electrical leaks in the system by providing a third path for leaking electricity to follow. In the event of an unsafe electrical condition, ground wires carry electricity back to the panel's neutral bus and into the earth through a *grounding rod* driven at least eight feet into the soil.

To put it simply without getting into vivid details, a grounded system should direct the leaking electricity into the ground, and hopefully *not* into the body of the unfortunate person touching a defective appliance or circuit. Even with a grounded system, always use caution and treat faulty electrical switches, appliances, and outlets with respect. If you fear that something is wrong, turn off the circuit breaker first before touching anything!

Another advantage to a grounded electrical system is the ability to place special outlets near a water source, such as a bathroom or kitchen sink. Most codes require that a receptacle called a *GFCI* (ground fault circuit interrupter) must be installed within six feet of any sink, tub, or other water source. A properly working GFCI will constantly monitor the hot, neutral, and ground wires of the circuit when an appliance is used near water, and if it senses anything other than a normal condition, it shuts down the circuit.

If correctly installed, one GFCI hooked up on the first outlet of a circuit can protect all the other outlets in the circuit. If you need only one receptacle protected, you can get a GFCI designed for just one outlet. Plug-in models may also be available, but check your local codes.

Finally, you can have *GFCI breakers* installed in the panel box with your other circuit breakers, and these will protect the entire circuit loop.

Codes require grounding wires on new electrical systems, but in older homes you may just have the two-wire power and neutral circuits. If you do, you have old, *ungrounded* electrical circuits, and they should be updated with new grounding wires. In many cases local codes may require grounding older electrical systems whether you want to or not!

Mapping Your Electrical System

When I used to go on service calls, nothing frustrated me more than opening up the breaker box for the home and seeing that there were no names for the circuits in the box! Or, just as bad, that the name tags for the circuits had fallen off or worn out. Either way, if your breaker box is not mapped out clearly, sooner or later this will cost you time and money. It's very expensive to pay a contractor to play guessing games with your circuits.

All homeowners need to ensure that their circuit breakers are clearly marked and labeled. Mapping your electrical system is necessary not only for normal service work but, more important, for emergencies! When a circuit needs to be shut down quickly, that's no time for you to be aimlessly flipping switches yelling out, "Did anything go off?"

The good news is that mapping your home's electrical circuits is a fairly easy job. The only skill you need is the ability to flip a switch and to be patient. The bad news is, it will take some time, and you'll need to find a helper for this job. The tools are pretty simple as well: some good labels and a laundry marker, a plug-in radio or lamp, and a pair of walkie-talkies that actually work. Cell phones are the best as long as you use them on free time!

First you need to delegate job responsibility. One person has to run around throughout the entire house with the lamp or radio, testing outlets and relaying information as to what is on or off. We'll call this person the "tester." The second person stands by the breaker box, flips switches, and labels each breaker. We'll call this person the "flipper." If possible, try to land the flipper job! For safety reasons, the flipper must

Before you start, make sure that any delicate electronic equipment, like TVs and computers, is turned off. Every circuit breaker will be flipped on and off several times at some point, and you don't want to take costly chances with electronics that may be damaged by power surges.

always switch breakers on and off with only one hand touching the box at a time. Keep the other hand at your side. Two hands touching different sections of the box at the same time can be unsafe!

Most circuits have multiple fixtures, but some should service only one appliance, so map out your appliance circuits first.

The kitchen is a good place to start, since that's where the majority of your appliances are located, such as dishwashers, disposers, and microwaves. Large appliances like electric ovens or clothes dryers should be on a 240-volt, high-voltage circuit. In the breaker panel, a 240-volt breaker will take up the space of two 120-volt breakers and have a *double toggle switch*, making them easy to identify. So with the "big"

appliances, try the "big" breakers in the panel first to save some time.

Have the tester person go to the kitchen and start up the dishwasher. As the dishwasher is running, the flipper person starts from the top of the circuit panel (below the main power shutoff) and flips the breaker-panel switches off and on, going in order down the line of breakers.

Communication is key. As soon as the tester hears the dishwasher stop, he or she must tell the flipper over the walkie-talkie to "hold up" at that breaker. Double-check by repeated flipping to ensure that you have found the dishwasher breaker, and then label that circuit "Dishwasher." Many boxes will have a number for a circuit breaker stamped on the panel. In that case use the number as well. Example: #4: dishwasher.

Do this same process for every appliance in your home, and before you know it, you'll have a circuit map for all your appliances! But you're not done. Now it's time to map out the circuits for all the lights and outlets in your home. This is basically the same process as mapping the appliances.

When the lights and/or receptacles go out in the area you're testing, isolate that breaker with the corresponding fixtures and outlets. For example, they can be marked "Master Bedroom Lights" or "Bathroom GFCI Outlets" or whatever area you find that a panel breaker services. Again, use numbers if you have them.

Once the entire house's circuits are mapped out and clearly labeled, you'll be amazed at how often you'll use the information now marked on the panel door and how much easier and safer all your electrical repair projects will be!

Resetting a Circuit Breaker

Appliances have a lot of breaker protection, but the most common place a breaker will trip is in the electrical service box of your home. It's very important that you map out and label your circuit breakers in the panel to simplify the resetting process.

If you experience a power failure while working in your kitchen, the first step is to confirm that the power is off only to the area of the kitchen that you're working in. Check other areas of the kitchen or go to another room and turn on a light. I have heard of homeowners getting frustrated at trying to reset breakers, not knowing that a power outage has occurred in the entire neighborhood!

Once you've confirmed that it's only a circuit in the kitchen that's out, try to determine what tripped the breaker. If you just plugged in an appliance, unplug it. If the dishwasher and microwave were both on at the same time, shut them

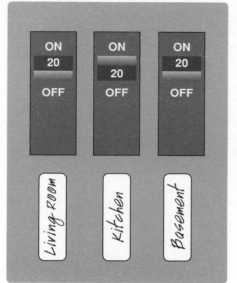

CIRCUIT BREAKER TRIPPED

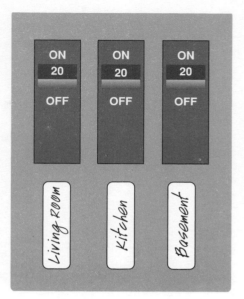

CIRCUIT BREAKER RESET

both off. The point here is to reset the breaker with a clean slate so it doesn't trip off again as soon as you reset it.

Next, go to your electrical panel and look for the breaker that's labeled for the circuit that has tripped, or look for a tripped breaker. A tripped breaker switch can be in the "off" position or between the "on" and "off" positions. To reset the breaker, hold one hand to your side while you stand on a dry, puddle-free floor. Flip the breaker to the "off" position and then back to the "on" position. Don't hold the switch in the "on" position.

The circuit should now be restored to normal power, and you can get back to work. Just stay within the safe working capacity of the circuit! If you hear loud buzzing from the breaker or if keeps shutting off as soon as you flip it on, keep it off and call a licensed electrician. The problem may not be a simple overload but a direct short in the wiring.

Changing a Fuse

Older homes may still have an old-style main service box that uses fuses instead of the modern circuit breakers. Basically, a fuse works along the same lines as a circuit breaker. But instead of tripping a switch into an "off" position, a fuse will completely burn out a metal element inside a glass tube when overloaded, to shut down the circuit.

Same as circuit breakers, fuses come in different amp ratings, and it's extremely important that you use the correct amp rating for your circuit. If you are moving into an older home that has a fuse box, it's a good idea to have your home inspector check the fuse panel for the proper fuses to use on each circuit and label each circuit with its correct amp size. Existing fuses may not always be the correct amp rating.

Unlike circuit breakers, which allow you to flip a switch and reuse the breaker, once a fuse is blown, you have to discard it. This means you always need to have new fuses on hand to replace the old fuses. As with breakers, the most common sizes for fuses will be 15 and 20 amps. Never replace a fuse with a different amp rating. Keep a variety of fuses on hand to ensure you can match amp sizes.

To replace a fuse, follow the same steps as for resetting a breaker,

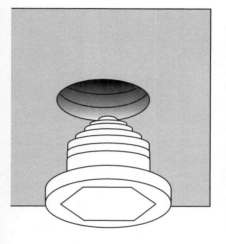

BLOWN FUSE
(SMOKEY, BLACKENED GLASS)

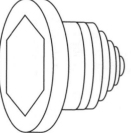

GOOD FUSE
(CLEAR GLASS)

NEW (20 AMP) FUSE—HANDLE BY RIM ONLY!

up to the point when you look into the service panel box. With fuses there won't be any switches in the box. Instead you'll see round, glass-topped stoppers, and each fuse is color-coded, with an amp rating printed on the fuse.

The color will help you identify the size fuse a little easier. For instance, 15-amp fuses usually have a blue stamp, 20-amp red/orange, and 30-amp green. Check your exact color and size to confirm. Then pick out the corresponding replacement fuses from your stock.

A blown fuse is easy to spot and will appear to have a black smudge or a burned look in the glass window. If you can change a lightbulb, you can change a blown fuse. With one hand at your side, standing on a dry floor, turn the old fuse counterclockwise and remove it. Get a new fuse with the correct-size amperage and turn it clockwise into the socket.

If new fuses keep blowing as soon as you change them or if you have a different electrical panel box setup, involving something other than breakers or fuses, consult a licensed electrician.

Resetting GFCI Outlets

GFCI stands for "ground fault circuit interrupters," and they are the silent saviors in a kitchen or anywhere that water and electricity can come in contact with each other. A GFCI is designed to detect unusual draws in electrical current and shut down the outlet.

A typical kitchen will have several outlets off one main GFCI outlet. So if the main GFCI outlet trips, all the outlets may go off in the kitchen. That can confuse some people. Why is every outlet off, yet none of the circuit breakers in the box are tripped? So it's important that you learn to identify a GFCI outlet and know how to reset it.

Since the late 1970s, GFCIs have started showing up as standard equipment in selected electrical circuits. Today they are required by code in just about every area of the country. If you live in an older home and have no GFCI protection, you need to bring your home up to date. Call a licensed electrician to check for and/or install GFCI protection.

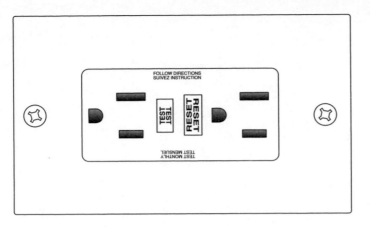

GFCIs can also be found on special circuit breakers in the service panel or on the plugs of common electrical appliances like hair dryers. But most of the time you'll find the GFCI breakers built into electrical outlets within six feet of sinks, tubs, or other water sources.

Wherever a GFCI is located, one common trait that they all usually share is "test and reset" buttons. This is very convenient, because testing the GFCI is recommended at least once a month. Plus, the buttons will give you practice on how to reset a GFCI if it ever trips.

To test and/or reset a GFCI outlet, simply press the "test" button, and the breaker should shut off the outlet. Reset the GFCI by pressing in the "reset" button, and power should be restored.

If an appliance trips a GFCI outlet, make sure you shut down the panel circuit breaker for that outlet before attempting to touch or unplug the appliance. Also, if the GFCI fails to reset after the appliance is removed and the panel breaker is back on, consult your electrician

Electrical Wires

Electrical wire is available in different grades and configurations, depending on the type of job that needs to be done. The most basic choice is *UF* which stands for *"underground feed"* wire, rated for outdoor use, or *NM*, and that stands for *non-metallic* covered wire used in dry indoor areas.

The choices get a little more complicated when it comes to the different wire *gauges* and *bundles*. Gauge refers to wire thickness, and bundle indicates how many and what type of wires are inside the sheathing. To make this less complicated, here are just a few of the most common types of wires you may have to work with in your home:

Ten-gauge wire: This heavy-duty wire can carry up to 30 amps.

Twelve-gauge wire: Commonly used and carries up to 20 amps.

Fourteen-gauge wire: Very common and carries up to 15 amps.

Eighteen-gauge wire: Low voltage only! Thermostats and doorbells.

BX cable: Metal wire casing required in exposed areas as per codes.

UF cable: Watertight wire sheathing rated for outdoor use per codes.

Two-wire NM 2G cable: Black, white, and ground wire all in one sheathing.

Three-wire NM 3G cable: Black, red, white, and ground wire in one sheathing.

Electrical System: Final Words

When in doubt about any electrical projects, call a licensed electrician!

PRO TIP

The lower the wire's gauge number, the thicker the wire will be, to carry more electricity. In most cases the information will be clearly marked on the wire casing. If you're not sure of the wire type or gauge, do not use it or work with it.

HVAC

The type of HVAC (heating, venting, air-conditioning) system you have will depend on the climate you live in. In very cold areas, the heating systems are powered by heavy-duty *boilers* with modest air-conditioning systems. In warm climates the heating system may be nothing more than a small backup *furnace* for a large air-conditioning system.

For now let's discuss heating only. A heating system is designed according to the size of the house, the design of the house, and the climate where the house is located. If you don't take all those factors into consideration, a heating system will not operate properly or efficiently, and anyone visiting your home may be greeted with a chilly reception.

Along with a good design, you also need an *energy source* to create heat. Most heating systems will operate with a fuel source, but some homes may simply use electricity to generate heat for the home.

Electrical current traveling through special baseboard heating elements will give off enough energy to heat a house. However, in very cold climates electric heat can be very costly to operate. Natural or propane gas and home heating oil are more efficient choices if you need to generate a lot of heat for a long period of time over the winter months.

Heating systems and equipment are rated by measuring units called *BTUs*. BTU stands for *"British thermal unit,"* and to put it simply, one BTU is equal to the amount of heat it takes to raise the temperature of one pound of water by one degree Fahrenheit.

One BTU is also equal to burning about 250 calories. So if you ran about a mile on a treadmill, you could theoretically burn off enough energy to provide your home's heating system with one BTU. An average rating for a boiler or furnace that supplies heat for a standard house can be around ninety thousand BTUs. So it would take an awful lot off running on a treadmill to heat a house!

Energy and Heat

Whether your heat comes from wood pellets burning in a special stove, solar panels on a roof, or geothermal water from deep in the ground, the heating industry is huge, and it seems there's always a new product out there every year that someone predicts will be the next hottest thing in home heating.

One heating product that came on the market many years ago did change the industry forever, and it's still the main and most-used control on any heating system. Nearly every home has at least one of these simple controls that can operate many complicated heating systems no matter what you use for energy.

Of course I'm talking about the *thermostat*, the magic dial with the numbers that automatically tells your heating system when to start up and when to shut down. No matter what type of heating system you have, they all rely on the thermostat to keep the house at an even, comfortable temperature. But usually that's where the similarities stop with heating systems.

Once you get past the thermostat, there are many different types of

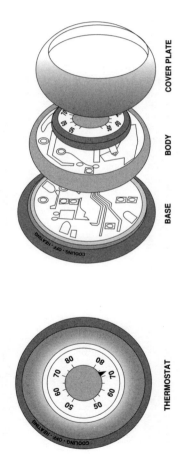

THERMOSTAT

COVER PLATE

BODY

BASE

heating systems and equipment to choose from in today's home-heating market. From different fuel types to water-based systems, it can get very confusing trying to figure out exactly what you have in your existing house or what you should choose to heat your new home.

Many of the new products are good ideas and may someday be the standard in home heating systems. However, I have noticed over the years that changes come slowly in the heating industry, and right now there are a few tried-and-true methods used for home heating. So I'm going to stay with the most popular and basic heating systems out there, and chances are you'll have one of these systems in your home.

Let's start off with the basic thing you need to know about heating, and that's the types of energy sources used to power standard home heating systems. The fuel or resources you use depend largely on the climate you live in and the availability of the energy to you.

Electric energy: As I mentioned, some homes use electricity for a heating source. Electric heat is fairly inexpensive to install and maintain, since the equipment is not complicated. But operating costs to run electric baseboard heating elements can be high. That's why you'll usually find electric heat in areas where the electricity rates are cheaper, in warmer climates, or in vacation homes that are not heated year-round.

To identify whether a house has electric heat, look for a high-voltage thermostat located in every room, which acts as an automatic switch to turn the heating elements on and off. Since the elements themselves supply the heat, another telltale sign of electric heat is that there is no central heating equipment for the home; each room has its own electric baseboard.

Electric heat also requires no *chimney* or *flue*, since no fuel is being burned. It's commonly used for houses with slab foundations, in small additions, or for supplemental heat in colder areas of a larger home.

Oil heat: Home heating oil is a refined fossil fuel that's very powerful and efficient to burn with the proper *oil burner*. Oil heat delivers a high rate of BTUs per gallon, which means you get a lot of bang for the buck! That's why oil heat is commonly used in the colder northern areas of the country. There's no mistaking that deep, forceful rumbling sound when an oil furnace or oil boiler fires up—it's music to my ears because that means it's working. When I know something is working, I'm always happy!

If a home has oil heat, there's usually one or two on-site oil-storage tanks in the basement. In some cases a larger oil tank may be buried outside in the ground. If a house does have a buried oil tank, local codes need to be checked to see if the tank may have to be removed. Many areas no longer allow in-ground oil tanks because of environmental concerns. Most older oil tanks are big, oblong, dirty-black steel drums turned on their sides. But newer tanks can be square, shiny metal tanks with special double linings.

Heating oil can easily be delivered by a local oil company to remote locations, making it very popular for rural homes with no public utilities. Most heating-oil companies also offer service contracts for every component in the heating system, making oil a very convenient option for the homeowner.

Natural gas: Natural gas, as the name says, is a gas extracted from the earth and refined for residential or commercial applications. It's used in the form of a light gas, but massive amounts can be transported to storage facilities in the form of a liquid called *LNG (liquefied natural gas)*.

It's a very clean-burning, efficient fuel that is basically odorless and colorless, but a strong odorant is added to natural gas so leaks can be readily identified. Most people don't even realize that the rotten-egg odor isn't natural gas's "natural" smell at all. On top of being an excellent choice for heating, natural gas is also a great fuel for cooking appliances and clothes dryers, making it an all-in-one energy source for many homes.

In populated areas natural gas can be connected to individual homes by means of an underground gas-pipeline system. Each home on the pipeline has its own gas meter to record the amount of natural gas used. One big advantage with a natural-gas energy system is that no scheduled deliveries are ever needed. Because of the direct hookup to a utility system, the gas is always there when you need it.

Propane gas: *LPG (liquefied petroleum gas)*, or propane gas, can be thought of as natural gas's country cousin. Propane gas is produced in part from natural-gas processing along with crude oil refining. A lot of the same characteristics of natural gas are also found in propane gas. The added odor, clean burning, and ease of storage and distribution are just a few of the shared advantages of both fuels. But the bottom line is that even with all the similarities, they are still two different types of fuel.

Propane is used mainly in rural areas that natural-gas utility companies do not service. Propane is the alternative to oil if the country homeowner wants a natural-gas type of heating system. Since propane in most cases is not supplied to a home through a pipeline system, a large propane-storage tank is set up on location and connected to the home. The LPG is then delivered and the tank filled regularly by a propane-gas company.

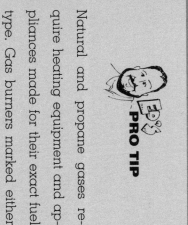

PRO TIP

Natural and propane gases require heating equipment and appliances made for their exact fuel type. Gas burners marked either for propane gas or natural gas must be used with that gas only!

Solar energy: This is a popular energy source for areas of the country where the conditions are just right to produce the required amount of heat needed from the sun's rays. It's easy to spot a house with solar heat—just look for the big flat panels on the roof aimed at the southern sky.

Solar is a true natural energy. The panels collect heat from the sun and circulate an exchange fluid through themselves and into the home. The heat is then transferred into large water tanks for evening use, when the sun is gone. The next day the process starts all over again. But as everyone knows, on cloudy days there's no sunlight available and often a backup energy source is needed.

Although the hot rays from the sun are free, solar heat does come at a price. Complete solar-energy systems needed to catch those rays and transfer the heat into a house can be very expensive.

Oil- and Gas-Burning Systems

Obviously, there are more energy sources out there for heating a home. For instance, fuels like wood and coal are extremely popular but not commonly used as a *system fuel*. In most cases wood and coal are burned in a stove or a fireplace, and even though a heat exchange does take place, these are not really thought of as a "heating system."

Heating systems for the most part are a series of automatic controls and equipment working together with a *self-feeding* fuel source. Think of a heating system as its own self-reliant engine. When the system is running properly, there should be very little outside effort needed from the homeowner to keep that heating engine going.

By far the most popular heavy-duty heating systems in today's homes are the oil- and natural- or propane-gas-burning systems. Most colder areas heat with oil or gas, and I'll explain the types of heating systems that run with these fuels.

The most common are the *water-based* and *air-based* heating systems. The heart and soul of the fuel-burning heating system is the *furnace or boiler*. This important piece of equipment is what generates the heat for the entire house. If your furnace or boiler stops running, you're out of heat, plain and simple. Don't ask me why, but if they do fail, it's usually in the middle of the night—on a holiday!

To cut down your chances of having a stressful heating emergency, once again you should follow the advice of that old saying "The best of-fense is a good defense." At the start of every season, have a licensed professional serviceperson clean and check your furnace or boiler.

One of the most frequently asked heating questions I hear is, what's the difference between a furnace and a boiler? A furnace and a boiler are two different kinds of heating equipment used for different types of home heating systems. While they can burn some of the same approved fuels, a furnace in general is used to generate *hot-air* based heat, and a boiler generates *hot-water* based heat. Along with using the same types of fuels, a furnace and a boiler share two other very important components: a *burner* and a *heat exchanger.*

A burner is the piece of equipment on a furnace or boiler that actually burns the fuel in the *firebox,* converting it into heat. Hence the name burner! Depending on the type of fuel used, the furnace or boiler will have an oil burner, a natural-gas burner, or a propane burner. The approved burner must be used with its approved fuel type. Burners are rated for different sizes and BTUs and should be chosen according to the heating power needed for the home.

The heat exchanger is the closed chamber where the heat from the burned fuel is exchanged into the ductwork or circulating water for the home. Hence the name heat exchanger! This sealed chamber not only transfers the burner heat safely into the home's heating system, but it also channels the wasted fuel gases out of the furnace or boiler and through the house flue, discharging it outside into the atmosphere.

Water- and Air-Based Systems

Steam heat: Steam heat was one of the first heating systems widely available to homeowners. You can always spot a steam system by its very large, accordion-shaped *radiators* that hiss and clang often. In the mid-1900s steam was the state-of-the-art industry standard for residential heating systems, and many of the original *steam loops* and radiators installed way back when are still in use today!

Steam heat has a reputation for being an outdated, inefficient, and uneven type of heat. In part that reputation goes back to the early days when installers did not know how to calculate *heat loads.* Bigger seemed better, so they just installed huge steam boilers and radiators. Since fuel was relatively cheap back then, it was thought best to oversize the heating system. If it got too hot, they simply opened a window! Now that's living large!

Today's steam boilers are smaller and more efficient than the old fuel-guzzling giants, and it's very common to install a new steam boiler onto an older steam-heating system. New or old, a steam boiler will have a built-in clear *viewing tube* to show the water level inside it. If the water level gets too low, more water must be added manually or with an autofill valve to keep the boiler half to three-quarters full. If too much water is added, the system can become *flooded* and not operate properly.

Steam heat works on a very simple principle. Think of the steam boiler as big bucket of water that's heated until it comes to a boil. Once steam is created inside the boiler, it rises into and fills a distribution piping system to radiate the heat. The pipes, or steam loop, divert the steam into radiators, where it is used for heat and vented off. Some steam will cool before it vents and condense into water, which drains back to the boiler, where it's reused.

Even though steam heating is an outdated system, it does have some advantages. For one thing, it's a very moist heat, and another upside is that many steam systems are set up to operate with no electricity, so in a power outage you'll still have heat! On the downside, older steam systems may have been installed with asbestos insulation wrap that needs to be inspected, addressed, and removed by a licensed professional only.

Hydronic heat: This is another water-based heating system, commonly referred to as *forced hot-water heat*. As the name says, water is forced through the boiler and piping system with a *circulator pump*. Hydronic heat and steam heat are both water-based systems, but there are major differences between the two types of heat.

Hydronic heat involves a *closed piping* system completely filled with water under low pressure, usually in the 15-to-20-psi range. Steam has water only in the lower two-thirds of the boiler, and the piping and radiators are filled with air when not in use. Efficient hydronic systems also operate with a water temperature of 140 degrees to 180 degrees Fahrenheit. Water for steam heat, of course, is heated to a boiling temperature of 212 degrees Fahrenheit.

Most forced hot-water systems use *baseboard radiation* to transfer the heat into the house. Baseboard radiators are fin-covered pipes inside a metal casing about seven inches high and attach to the walls at floor level. Hydronic heat can be used with other types of radiators, with heating coils, and even in the floor with *radiant heat* piping. Radiant heating loops, however, will operate with a lower water temperature of around 98 degrees Fahrenheit.

Hydronic heat works by circulating hot water through piping loops called *heating zones*. Each zone will take care of its own section of the home, and small houses may have only one zone. When a zone calls for heat through its zone thermostat, the circulator pump starts and the boiler fires up.

The hydronic boiler usually maintains a water temperature of at least 140 degrees Fahrenheit and will continue to fire until it tops off at about 180 degrees. The boiler will then stop firing to save energy, but the circulator will continue to run and circulate the hot water through the zone until the area is heated and the zone shuts down. If the zone requires more heat, the boiler starts up again when the water temperature drops to 140 degrees, and the process begins over again. Multiple zones can operate at the same time.

Hydronic systems are a complex series of electronic relays, pressure-relief valves, autofill valves, and safety-control limits. But, surprisingly, it is a very reliable and powerful heating system. Also, because of separate zone controls and recirculating heat loops it's a very efficient heating system.

Air-based heating and cooling: A hot-air heating system uses *duct-work* feed and returns to heat the home and relies on air instead of water to make the heat exchange. Air-based systems deliver the heat through shutterlike *registers* located at the ends of the duct feed trunks. Registers are usually located in the floor or ceiling of a room.

Hot-air-based systems work well in less severe climates, since the heating furnace and air-conditioning system can operate with the same ductwork. This saves on initial installation costs in areas that need full-time air conditioning, and it also allows an easy switch-over between heating and air-conditioning systems with only one thermostat.

Hot-air furnaces can operate with oil, natural gas, or propane gas, and the heat exchanger works by channeling the home air through a chamber with baffles and fins, where it is spread around a closed firebox that is heated by the burning fuel. As the home air passes over the hot box, a heat transfer takes place, and the hot air is now used to heat the home. The firebox connects directly to the flue, and the wasted gases leave the home.

The duct system uses a large fan called an *air handler* to circulate air through the system. The air handler draws air from the duct returns on the system and pulls it through an *air filter* before it moves it into the furnace. From there hot air is moved into the feed ducts for heating. For air conditioning, the furnace is off and the air moves through an A/C cooling coil and then to the feed ducts with cool air.

Some air-based systems in milder climates can use a "cool" piece of electrical equipment called a *heat pump* instead of a furnace. A heat pump is basically an air conditioner with a two-way valve that can let it run forward or backward. In one direction it warms the home air ducts and discharges cool waste; in the other direction it cools the home air ducts and discharges warm waste. A heat pump simply shuffles energy back and forth!

Choosing Heating Systems

The type of heating system needed for your home will depend mostly on the climate you live in and the industry standard for your area.

Wet or hydronic heating systems like baseboard or radiant heat are usually the choice in colder climates because of their efficiency and heating power. More temperate climates may go with hot air, because it switches easily from heating to air conditioning with the flip of a switch. Finally, warm areas may need just an electrical backup heating element for a few chilly nights.

HVAC Systems: Final Words

Remember, if you are not happy with your present heating system, in most cases you *can* change from one to another. For instance, a lot of people with steam heat change over to forced hot-water hydronic heat for the energy savings and ease of use. However, changing systems is costly and invasive to a home, because many of the components have to be installed in walls, floors, and ceilings. So make sure you will get a payback from the new system in energy savings or value to your home before you make an expensive switch.

BATHROOM WORK

BATHROOM CLOGS   61

Sinks   62

Clearing lavatory sink clogs   62

Clearing lavatory trap clogs   63

Clearing lavatory drain clogs   64

Toilets   66

Clearing a toilet with a force cup plunger   66

Clearing a toilet with a closet auger   67

Bathtub and shower   68

Clearing tub and shower drains   68

Cleaning the tub shoe   70

Cleaning the tub shoe overflow and trip lever   70

Plunging the tub   71

Clearing the shower stall trap   71

Plunging the shower drain   72

TOILETS   73

The three most common flushing systems   73

Common toilet repairs   75

Replacing the ballcock   76

Replacing the handle   77

Replacing the flapper   78

TOILET MAINTENANCE TIPS   79

Installing a toilet   79

BATHROOM SINKS AND FAUCETS   86

Lavatory sinks   86

Faucet holes in lav sinks   87

Quick-install faucets   89

Installing a quick-install faucet   93

SHOWERHEADS AND PERSONAL SHOWERS   96

Replacing a standard showerhead   97

Installing a standard personal shower   100

TUB AND SHOWER GRAB BARS   104

Style and location   104

Installing the grab bar   105

BATHROOM EXHAUST FANS   108

Fan maintainenace   109

Changing the fan lightbulb   110

Cleaning the fan and housing   111

Changing the fan motor   111

Fan airflow   112

Ed's words of wisdom on bathrooms: *The bathroom is one of man's great inventions and will always rise to the level of the society for which it serves!*

THE BATHROOM IS "THE" ROOM

If you sat down and tried to design a new room for a house that used every system a home has to offer, a room that could be updated easily, and one that people would want to wait in line just to enter, you could not design a better room than the bathroom!

The ancestor of our modern bathroom was the outhouse, which was basically a hole in the ground covered by a small shed that offered privacy to a shy society. As simple as the outhouse was, it did the job well for its time. Today in some remote areas, outhouses are still used, and from a plumber's point of view it's a very reliable piece of equipment that's virtually maintenance free!

As our society has evolved, so have our bathrooms, and nowadays they can be pretty complicated spaces and require constant maintenance. Believe it or not, computers have even started to find their way into our showers, sinks, and toilets. While past plumbers could solve bathroom problems by burning them down and digging a new hole, tomorrow's plumbers will have to master electronics as well as plumbing to stay in business!

But enough about the past and future of our bathrooms. We need to deal with our present bathrooms and learn how to keep them updated and running properly. In this chapter I've compiled some information and a list of the most common bathroom projects and repairs you may encounter.

Along with firsthand experience, I also included my "tricks of the trade" on what I've found will work best to keep your bathroom up and running!

BATHROOM CLOGS

The dreaded bathroom clog is the number-one problem my plumbing customers have hired me to solve over the many years that I've done professional home-improvement calls.

Even if you are a skilled do-it-yourselfer, a bathroom clog is one of those jobs you just don't *want* to do yourself! My advice? Get over it. Nowadays homeowners can't afford to be picky about the jobs they prefer to do and don't prefer to do.

Okay, I agree that the majority of bathroom clogs are not for the faint of heart and can be pretty nasty to deal with. I must confess that I've been humbled and embarrassed by most of my bathroom-clog jobs—not because of what I had to deal with to clear them but because of my customers' reactions to me after I completed the job. Things like avoiding shaking my hand or looking at me with total fear and disrespect—that hurt my feelings! I made up for this by raising my prices a bit so I'd feel better about myself. The lesson here is to always appreciate and respect your plumber—or else it can cost you!

To stop fearing the bathroom clog, you need to understand that a bathroom is the perfect environment to breed clogs. What with showering, shaving, and—of course—nature calls, it's normal that clogs will develop from time to time, so don't panic when they do happen.

After you get your first hands-on experience with a good-size bathroom clog, every clog after that will seem a bit less stressful. Trust me, you'll get to a point where nothing that bubbles up out of a drain or toilet will faze you. Once you get over your anxiety about working with bathroom clogs, the job itself can be very easy.

In fact, clearing most bathroom clogs is a very simple process and can be one of those home-improvement jobs that may save you a lot of money with little time invested. However, you will need to make a small investment in some specialty tools we discussed in the "Tools" chapter (see p. 1). With a cup plunger, a force cup plunger, a grabbing tool, a drain auger, closet auger, and some knowledge of how each tool works, you can tackle most common bathroom clogs. Remember that bathroom clogs are smaller clogs that usually happen in the fixture or fixture trap. If you have a main house clog or severe clogs in the drain lines located inside the walls or floor, chances are you'll need a professional.

Sinks

Clearing Lavatory Sink Clogs

Bathroom sinks are very prone to hair clogs. When you mix the end results of shaving, combing your hair, and using soap and toothpaste, all going down a small drain, something bad is bound to happen. The good news is that many pop-up assemblies on bathroom

---

TROUBLE NOTE

Also, do not attempt any work yourself on a drain or fixture if chemicals have been used and the clog does not clear. Plumbing fixtures and drains full of chemicals can cause safety concerns while plunging and/or dismantling drain traps.

faucets are designed to catch a lot of this debris before it gets into the sink trap.

To clear a lav sink pop-up clog, you first need to remove the stopper from the pop-up assembly. Some sink stoppers simply pull out, while most are locked in place with a ball rod, and some disassembly of the pop-up assembly is required to remover the stopper from the drain hole.

Tools and Materials Needed: Small slip-joint pliers, small cup plunger, and the grabbing tool.

Push down the pop-up rod to lift the stopper. Then remove the ball rod collar nut from the pop-up body and slide the ball rod back till the rod slides out of the stopper, and pull the stopper out. With the stopper removed, reattach the ball rod and nut to the body.

Do a visual inspection of the stopper and drain hole. Clean any debris off the stopper and remove any clog or debris from the drain hole with the grabbing tool. Run some water and plunge the sink a few times with the cup plunger. Reinstall the stopper and test the drain.

Clearing Lavatory Trap Clogs

If the pop-up assembly is clean and the water in the sink still does not drain, the next step is to "pressure-plunge" the trap. With the stopper removed or open, place a wet rag over the sink "overflow" hole, this is the trick the pro's use to create pressure. Vigorously plunge the sink drain with the cup plunger while holding the wet rag over the hole. This may clear the trap. If not, your next step is to open up the trap.

Most traps will have access fittings to enter the trap. Many will have a large plug at the base of the trap bend, but most will have two large collar nuts on each side of the bend for complete trap removal. Also, some traps are PVC plastic and some chrome/brass.

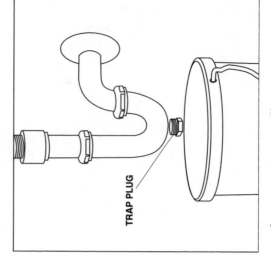

TRAP PLUG

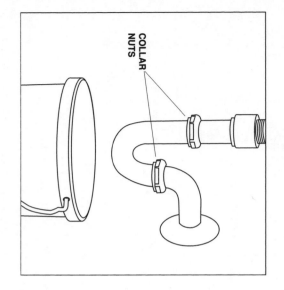

COLLAR
NUTS

Tools and Materials Needed: Slip-joint pliers, grabbing tool, shallow bucket, safety glasses, gloves, and rags.

Again, make sure there are no standing chemicals in the sink or drain. In most cases there will be water in the sink and drain lines if you have a clog, and it will spill out under the sink area once the trap is opened.

Put on gloves and place a bucket under the trap bend. If you have the type of trap with an access plug at the base of the trap bend, use the slip-joint pliers to loosen the plug until you can twist it with your fingers. Slowly twist the plug till water starts to dribble out of the trap. Allow the water to drain out completely from the sink and trap.

Once the waste water is removed from the drain line, remove the plug from the trap. You can now access the trap bend hole with the grabbing tool. Move the grabbing tool around the inside of the trap and clear out any debris or obstructions. Reinstall the trap plug and test.

If you have a trap with large collar nuts on each side of the bend, loosen both nuts and allow the trap to drain. Once it's drained, remove both nuts from the trap and empty the remaining water into the bucket. Reinstall the trap plug and test.

Clear and clean out the inside of the trap bend with the grabbing tool and a rag. Reinstall the trap bend and test.

Clearing Lavatory Drain Clogs

If you clear the pop-up and trap and your sink still drains slowly, there may be a problem in the lav sink's drain line. The waste pipe starts after the trap bend and runs inside the bathroom walls or floor before tying in to the main bathroom drain line.

Most lav sink drain lines are usually no larger than an inch and a half in diameter and under fifteen feet in length, so the handheld drain auger should work well to clear this line.

Tools and Materials Needed: Along with the same tools and safety equipment needed to access and remove a lav trap, you'll also need a handheld drain auger.

To use the drain auger, first open the access plug or remove the trap as we described earlier. With the trap opened or removed you can insert the drain auger through the access hole up into the lav drain at the back of the trap or into the open drain line itself.

The drain auger has a springlike hook at the tip of the auger coil. Feed the coil into the drain, lock it, and turn the auger drum clockwise to spin the coil. Repeat this process until the coil passes through the clog; the hook end can usually catch the debris in the line.

To remove the auger from the drain line, gently pull the coil backward while feeding the coil back into the auger drum. Make sure that you have the bucket and rags at the drain opening and that you're wearing rubber gloves, because in most cases a nasty black slime will come out with the auger. Once you clear the lav drain, reinstall the trap and test the sink.

Chances are that by cleaning out the pop-up assembly and/or the sink trap and/or the drain line, your bathroom sink should drain like it's brand new! However, there can still be a hidden clog in the sink, vent, drain, or main line that you missed. Or the clog can be so massive that normal hand tools and techniques will not work. If this is the case, you'll have to call in a professional with industrial-strength power augers!

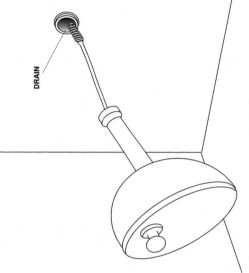

DRAIN

Toilets

For obvious reasons, the toilet can produce some of the nastiest clogs that you'll ever face in the bathroom. But the good news is that toilet clogs are some of the easiest to clear!

That's because the toilet trap and discharge-hole opening are usually smaller than the larger toilet drain line under the floor. The rule of thumb is, if it makes it through the toilet, it should make it through the main drain. So if your toilet clogs, it's likely that the clog is in the toilet itself and the house drain line should be clear.

With this knowledge, let's focus our attention on the toilet bowl itself. To clear a clogged toilet, you have two weapons to choose from: For starters I recommend you try a force cup plunger. If that doesn't work, you can try a toilet auger for heavy-duty clogs.

Clearing a Toilet with a Force Cup Plunger

It's very important that you use a *force cup plunger* when working with toilets—that's what the plumbers use! A regular cup plunger does not fit a toilet drain properly and, more important, will not give you good suction power. A force cup plunger has a built-in rubber funnel that fits into most toilet traps.

For common toilet clogs, where the toilet is flushing slowly or the water has not reached the top of the bowl rim, the force cup should work fine. Gently insert the plunger into the bowl and work the funnel end of the plunger into the bowl's trap hole. Once the funnel end is locked in place, slowly push the air out of the bell of the plunger to create a vacuum seal. The professional trick is to generate good suction inside the trap by sharply pulling the plunger back. Most toilet clogs are cleared by pulling back on the plunger, not by pushing on it.

When a toilet clogs up, the water in the bowl puts constant pressure on the clog, wedging it in place. If you use suction to pull the clog backward, it should break up the clog while the standing water washes it down the drain. Pushing on a clog may just compact it.

Clearing a Toilet with a Closet Auger

If you've tried plunging and plunging your toilet without any success, it may be time to call in the "big gun." A closet auger takes toilet clog removal to another level.

Instead of relying on a nice soft plunger to create a vacuum, the closet auger uses brute force to break through most clogs. It also has a special hook at the end to catch large debris.

I've personally pulled out hundreds of objects hopelessly stuck in toilets with a closet auger. When you get good with this tool, you can actually feel and hook the debris with the auger, like a fisherman reeling in a trout.

Also, since you're dealing with a thin coil and not a bulky plunger, even if the water level in the bowl has come up to the rim, you can usually work on the clog without splashing toilet water over the edge.

The downside is that a closet auger is a difficult tool to master, and because of the steel coil it's very easy to scratch the surface of the bowl. It's also possible for the auger to break the porcelain trap inside the toilet. If you don't use this tool with caution, you can make more trouble for your bathroom than the clog itself!

Be sure you have on your gloves and safety glasses, and follow your auger manufacturer's instructions for use. Unhook the auger from the top of the housing. Pull the crank handle out of the housing, and the auger snake will recoil into the housing while the crank shaft is exposed.

At the base of the housing is a curved end with a rubber sleeve to protect the toilet bowl's finish. Slowly insert the curved end into the trap opening. Hold the housing handle with one hand and the crank with the other. Your hands will be spread apart at this point.

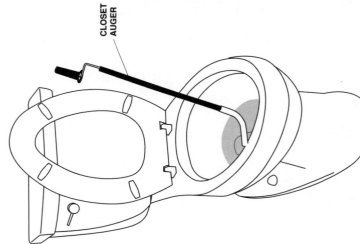

CLOSET AUGER

Gently but firmly turn the crank clockwise while pushing the crank shaft down. The auger should go up and into the bowl trap, and the toilet should clear at this point. Pull the crank shaft back up and out of the housing, remove the auger from the bowl, and test the toilet. If you have trouble using this tool, stop and call a professional plumber.

Bathtub and Shower

We all know how easily a lav sink can clog up. Well, just imagine a lav sink so big that you can climb into it and wash your entire body instead of just your face. How badly would *that* sink clog up?

You don't have to imagine this scenario, because your bathtub and shower are basically nothing more than oversize sinks. And like all plumbing fixtures, they have traps, and the traps for tub and shower units are notorious for catching debris and clogging frequently.

When it comes to tub and shower clogs, drain protection is your best bet. The main reason for tub and shower clogs is that hair (especially long hair) mixed with soap will eventually find its way into the trap through a standard tub and shower drain strainer.

So if you want to avoid most hair clogs, the solution is to catch the hair before it enters the drain trap. This can be done easily by purchasing a finer hair strainer that fits over your existing one. Local home centers will usually carry a few different models to fit most drain setups and they're very inexpensive.

Without a hair strainer to protect your drains, you may have to deal with a clog in your tub or shower. The good news is, most tub and shower drains can be cleaned out. I'm about to tell you how to do it properly.

Clearing Tub and Shower Drains

Tools and materials needed: Your basic hand tools, grabbing tool, cup plunger, gloves, glasses, and rags.

As always, don't try to open up or plunge any drains or traps if chemicals have been used and the fixture has not drained. In that case call a professional.

It's happened to all of us at one time or another. You're taking a shower, and slowly the water starts to rise in the tub. Before you know it, you're up to your ankles in gray, soapy water. You don't have to be a rocket scientist to figure out that you now have a clogged tub drain!

The typical panic reaction is to plunge the drain. But before you go plunger crazy, your best course of action is to see if you can locate and remove the clog from your "tub shoe."

The tub shoe (also called a tripwaste) is the drain, overflow, and lever assembly that allows you to open and close the tub drain. There are two basic types of tub shoes—cylindrical (A) or pop-up (B)—and both can be cleaned out.

When clearing tub and shower clogs, professional plumbers remove as much hair and debris as possible from the fixture drain before using a plunger. Plunging a hair clog can push it deeper into the house drains and may cause a clog in the main line.

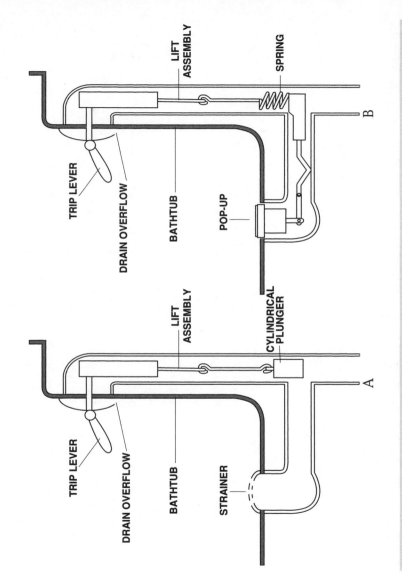

TRIP LEVER

DRAIN OVERFLOW

LIFT ASSEMBLY

BATHTUB

STRAINER

CYLINDRICAL PLUNGER

A

TRIP LEVER

DRAIN OVERFLOW

LIFT ASSEMBLY

SPRING

BATHTUB

POP-UP

B

The good thing about working on tub shoes is that many times you get a two-for-one-deal. To clean a shoe, you also have to work on and readjust the trip lever and rod. So if you were having problems with a lever or tub stopper not working properly, this will get fixed as well!

Cleaning the Tub Shoe: Most tub shoe drains will be one of two styles: a pop-up stopper type located in the drain hole itself or a strainer screen over the drain hole, with a cylindrical plunger/stopper inside the shoe.

POP-UP TYPE

To clean a pop-up type, pull the lever so the pop-up stopper pops up, grab the stopper by the edges, and pull it from the drain hole. Clean any debris from the stopper itself and use your grabbing tool to locate and remove debris from the drain hole.

CYLINDRICAL TYPE

To clean a cylindrical type, remove the center screw and/or pull off the drain strainer cover with the appropriate screwdriver for your style of tub shoe. Clean out the strainer holes and, again using the grabbing tool, reach into the open drain hole and clean out any debris. Often you'll find a clump of wet hair in the shoe drain assembly.

Once the stopper or strainer and tub shoe drain line are cleaned out, put everything back in place and move to the overflow.

Cleaning the Tub Shoe Overflow and Trip Lever: Access to the tub overflow is through the trip lever and cover plate, located usually just below the tub filler spout. To remove the tripwaste, first use a screwdriver to remove the two large flathead cover plate screws on either side of the lever.

Gently pull out the trip waste rod assembly from the overflow tube and inspect it for debris. Lift rods for the pop up-type tub shoes should have a spring at the end, and this is what will usually catch hair clogs. Remove any debris from the rod and spring.

Tub shoes that have a strainer at the drain use a cylindrical stopper inside the overflow tube. Check the cylinder at the end of the lift rod for debris, clean, and apply plumber's grease to the cylinder.

Before putting the trip lever and rod assemblies back into the overflow tube, insert the grabbing tool inside the tube to search for any remaining debris. Check out the condition of the trip lever and rods as well, and replace any broken or worn-out parts.

Finally, put the trip lever, rods, cylinder, or spring and cover plate assembly back in place and check the adjustment of the trip lever. Check to be sure that the cylinder or pop-up stopper opens and closes completely. If not, make any necessary adjustments to the rod adjustment mechanism. Believe it or not, many slow tub drains can be blamed on the fact that the tub drain stopper doesn't open up all the way! Once the trip lever lift rods and stoppers work properly, reinstall the screws on the cover plate.

Plunging the Tub: With the tub shoe cleaned out, now you can plunge the drain to remove any remaining debris from the trap without the worry of pushing more hair clogs into it.

Fill the tub with some water and hold a wet rag over the overflow hole to create pressure and suction while plunging. Make sure the drain stoppers are open and work the water back and forth with a cup plunger till the tub drains freely. If cleaning out the tub shoe and then power plunging does not work, you should consult with a plumber.

Cleaning the Shower Stall Trap: A shower stall trap and drain is larger and more accessible in most cases than a tub drain. Even though this makes it sound like an easier job, you still need to follow the same rules; Don't work on a shower drain if chemicals have been

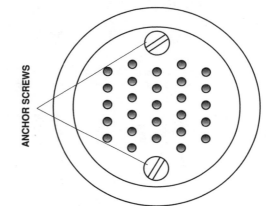

ANCHOR SCREWS

PRO TIP

Bathroom hair and clogs are normal. The trick is to identify them and clear them while they're small. If left unchecked, a little wet mouse can turn into a big rat!

used, and clean out the trap before attempting to plunge the drain!

To get access to the trap, simply remove the two large screws at the floor drain that hold the strainer in place. Once the screws are removed, gently pry off the strainer from the drain housing. When the strainer is removed, you now have open access to the trap.

Shower drains and traps are usually two inches in diameter, which gives you plenty of room to insert the grabbing tool and grab hold of any hair and soap clogs. The handy thing about hair clogs is that they tend to "ball up," and if you grab just part of the clog with the tool and pull gently, the entire hair clog will come out at once. Plumbers call a small hair clog like this a wet mouse. Yuk!

Plunging the Shower Drain: With the strainer removed and the shower trap cleared, you can now plunge the shower trap and drain line. Place the cup plunger over the open drain hole and run some water in the shower till you have about an inch of water in the shower base.

Shut off the water and remove the plunger from the drain hole so water enters the drain. Time it so that when the water fills the trap and drain, you put the plunger back over the drain and start to plunge.

Since there is no overflow piping on shower stalls, the plunger's suction and pressure go right to the drain line. Vigorously plunge the drain line while allowing more water from the stall to enter the drain. Once the water drains out freely, reinstall the strainer. If cleaning the shower trap and then plunging doesn't work, consult a plumber.

TOILETS

The toilet is the most used bathroom fixture and the main reason small bathrooms were first added to houses! Thus was spawned a booming bathroom industry, and many of today's bathrooms look more like living rooms, with the toilet hidden away in a small closet area. Not much respect for such an important fixture!

The flushing system for a toilet is like a car engine. Just as cars have many kinds of engines for different types of automobiles, there are several types of flushing systems that run different types of toilets. You have your "economy models," "sports cars," and "luxury sedans." If you're thinking of installing a new toilet, the first thing you have to decide is what type of toilet will work best for you and your family.

There are three popular and practical flushing systems on the market today. Below is a description of each one to help make your choice of toilets very easy. Just pick the one that best matches your lifestyle and budget, and then, as they say, you'll be good to go!

The three most common flushing systems:

Gravity flush: A gravity toilet is by far the most popular flushing system on the market, the "economy model" toilet. They're affordable, easy to install and maintain, and give a good flush with the current regulation 1.6 gallons of water or less.

Think of a gravity-flush toilet like an aquarium. It holds water in a square tank. The water fills the tank through the "ballcock," or fill valve, and just sits in the tank waiting for someone to push the handle. When the toilet is flushed, the "flapper" opens up and gravity pulls the water out of

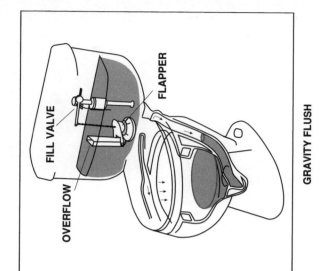

OVERFLOW
FILL VALVE
FLAPPER

GRAVITY FLUSH

the hole in the bottom of the tank and flushes the bowl. Then the entire flush cycle starts all over again.

The advantage of a gravity flushing system is that gravity is a constant force of nature and you get a good, steady flush every time, even if you have very low water pressure. The disadvantage is that because gravity is a constant, but specific, force of nature, there are limits to the flushing power a gravity system can generate.

Air-assisted flush: This system is sometimes called a *pressure-lite* toilet. It's very cool and could be considered the "sports car" of toilets. The way it works is truly simple and amazing. Instead of filling an open tank with water like the gravity flush, a pressure-lite toilet fills a closed and sealed tank with water. As the chamber fills, it traps a layer of air at the top of the tank. If the water pressure is the normal 45 to 75 psi, that means that the trapped air pressure is also in the range of 45 to 75 psi. When you push the handle, the pressurized air pushes the water out of the tank at a very high speed, creating a powerful, fast flush!

The big advantage of an air-assisted flush is that, like gravity toilets, no electricity is required, and air-assisted models can deliver a more powerful flush than gravity-flush toilets with even less water.

On average, pressure-lite toilets use 1.1 to 1.4 gallons per flush. The disadvantage of air-assisted toilets is that they can be a little noisier than gravity toilets, and if you have low water pressure, you cannot generate a very strong flush.

Power-assisted flush: Sometimes called a *power-lite* toilet, this flushing system is definitely the "luxury sedan" of toilets. But like all luxury

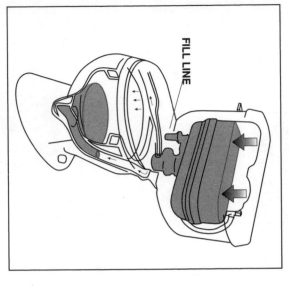

FILL LINE

AIR-ASSISTED FLUSH

models it does come with a high-end price tag. The tank has a built-in heavy-flow pump that takes the water from the tank and actually pumps it into the bowl at a high rate of speed, which gives the toilet incredible flushing power with very little noise.

Because it does not rely on trapped air pressure, this flush is like a gravity setup and will deliver powerful flushes in a house with low water pressure. Since it's also an assisted flush, it will be a more powerful flush, like compressed-air systems, but very quiet because of the smooth-running pump. So you get the best of both worlds in one toilet!

Another advantage is that because these toilets use electricity, some models have two-stage flushing buttons. The first button will deliver a full 1.6-gallon flush when needed, and the second button will deliver a smaller flush of 1 gallon for extra water savings. The disadvantage to a pump-assisted toilet is that since the toilet pump requires electricity to run, you will need to have a special GFCI (ground fault circuit interrupter) electrical outlet installed next to the toilet. Also, if the power goes out, the toilet cannot flush unless you pour a bucket of water into the bowl.

Common Toilet Repairs

Even a fairly new toilet can still develop flushing problems. Repairing newer toilets instead of replacing them may be a better decision. Most gravity-flush toilets are very simple fixtures once you look under the lid.

The three main flushing controls in the toilet tank are the ballcock (commonly called the fill valve), the flush handle, and the flapper. Most toilet problems will be traced back to one or all of these controls, and

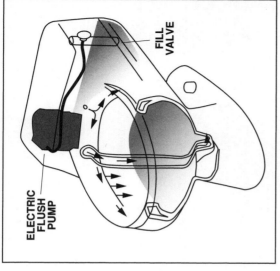

ELECTRIC FLUSH PUMP

FILL VALVE

POWER-ASSISTED FLUSH

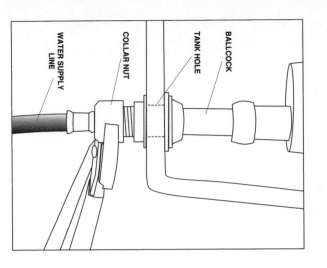

WATER SUPPLY LINE

COLLAR NUT

TANK HOLE

BALLCOCK

the good news is that these problems are very easy to troubleshoot and repair!

Replacing the Ballcock

If your toilet runs constantly and you notice that the water level in your tank is so high that water constantly runs down the overflow tube inside the tank, chances are your ballcock is not shutting down completely and should be replaced.

Tools and Materials Needed: Sponge and bucket, adjustable wrench, slip-joint pliers, replacement ballcock, and flexible toilet-supply line.

Shut off the water to the toilet and flush the water out of the toilet tank. Soak up the remaining tank water with the sponge and bucket. Completely disconnect and discard the old water-supply line with the adjustable wrench and slip-joint pliers.

Under the tank where the water line connects to the toilet is a large threaded fitting with a thin, flat nut holding the ballcock in place. Remove that flat nut—if you're working from above, since the nut is upside down, you'll need to turn the nut clockwise to loosen it. With the nut removed, the ballcock assembly can now be pulled up and out of the tank. Make sure to remove the small fill line from the overflow tube as well.

That's it. The old ballcock is gone, and now it's time to install the new one! Prep the seals and new ballcock according to the instructions supplied with it and insert it into the tank hole. Get the new thin, flat nut and tighten into place (don't overtighten!). Install the new flexible toilet water-supply line, turn on the water and set the water level for your toilet according to the ballcock instructions.

Don't forget to install the new fill line from the ballcock into the overflow tube!

Replacing the Handle

If the handle breaks, the toilet will not flush. First, take off the tank lid to confirm that the handle is in fact broken. Many times the handle will be fine and the problem is simply that the chain leading to the flapper has fallen off. If that's the case, just hook the chain back onto the handle. If the handle is broken, you'll need to know the make and model of your toilet in order to get the right one. Make and model numbers of a toilet can usually be found stamped inside the tank.

Tools and Materials Needed: Small slip-joint pliers and your handle kit.

Shut down the toilet's water valve and carefully pull up on the flapper flushing chain. If the handle is broken into pieces, make sure that no debris drains into the bowl. Once the water is out of the tank, remove any pieces and disconnect any handle parts still left on the toilet chain.

Remove the old handle from the toilet tank by taking off the handle's collar nut on the inside of the tank. Remember, you are actually standing behind this nut, so it can appear to be a reverse-threaded nut. Remove the collar nut and remaining handle assembly from the handle hole in the tank.

Slide the new handle shaft through the tank hole, then into the tank and mount it into the hole. Now slide the collar nut over the handle shaft from the inside of the tank and screw the nut onto the handle threads. Don't overtighten the nut! Finally, connect

PRO TIP

It's always best to get the handle made specifically for your toilet, but there are universal replacement handles available that fit many types of toilets. If you have trouble finding your make and model, you can try one of these handles first. Chances are it will work with your toilet.

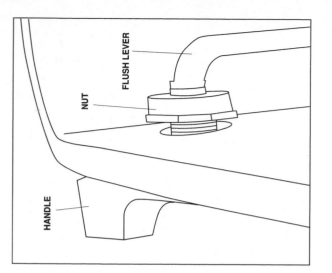

HANDLE

NUT

FLUSH LEVER

the flushing chain to the appropriate hole in the handle, making sure the chain has about a quarter to a half inch of play in every direction. Turn on the water and test-flush the toilet.

Replacing the Flapper

Okay, it's true that "flapper" is a funny name for a toilet part, but when your flapper goes bad, we're talking serious water waste! If you've ever heard your toilet flush by itself—or what we pros call a "phantom flush"—odds are it was a bad flapper causing the tank to loose water.

Think of the flapper like a cork on an upside-down wine bottle. The flapper is the rubber seal that holds all the water in the toilet tank. If your flapper develops a leak, the water will constantly run into the bowl, and when the water level in the tank drops too low, the ballcock will refill the tank, causing the phantom flush. This goes on

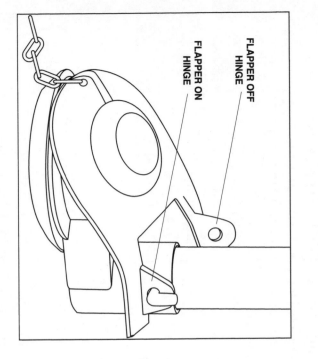

FLAPPER OFF HINGE

FLAPPER ON HINGE

twenty-four hours a day, wasting huge amounts of water!

Another flapper-related problem is a flapper that will not stay up to complete the toilet flush, forcing you to stand there holding the handle down to get a proper flush. In this case the flapper may also need to be changed.

Tools and Material Needed: Usually you won't need tools to change a flapper. All you need is your new flapper.

Even though changing a flapper is an easy job and can usually be accomplished in a matter of minutes, there is a tricky aspect to this job, and that's finding the right flapper. There are dozens of flappers on the market, and you need your exact match to do the job right. So here's my foolproof way to change a flapper. The "Ed method" will take a little more time, but trust me, it will save a lot of frustration!

First, shut off the toilet water valve and drain the water out of the tank. Now disconnect the flapper's flushing chain from the toilet handle. On each side of the flapper's hinge holes, there should be hinge posts mounted on the overflow tube. Slide the flapper off each mounting post and remove the flapper.

Take the old flapper that you just removed right down to your local home center. (Warn everyone in the house that the toilet is shut off for a bit.) With your old flapper in hand, it's now a very easy process to go through the entire flapper selection and find your toilet's twin flapper!

Get the new flapper and install it in the opposite order from how you removed it. Slide the hinge holes over each mounting post and attach the flush chain to the toilet handle. It's always important to leave the proper slack in the chain so that the flapper closes completely and pulls up all the way when the handle is pressed. The last step is to turn on the water, fill the tank, and test-flush.

TOILET MAINTENANCE TIPS

Regular inspections are the trick to keeping your toilet in good working order. For instance, flappers do not fail overnight—it can take months for a flapper to swell up and break down. From time to time, lift the tank lid and give all the components a good visual inspection.

When cleaning the inside of your toilet tank, be very careful not to hit or bang any of the components. And as far as tank cleaning goes, don't use any tank chemicals or additives that can damage rubber seals, or else you'll be repairing your toilet constantly!

Installing a Toilet

If your current toilet needs constant repair, you should consider replacing. First, you'll need to decide if you want a one-piece toilet or a two-piece toilet. As the names imply, a one-piece toilet comes complete with the tank built into the bowl, while a two-piece toilet comes in two sections, and you'll have to connect the tank to the bowl yourself.

Since one-piece toilets are built as a single component, they're bigger and heavier and require two people to move and install. If you're working alone or want to work with something lighter, with smaller components, I recommend a two-piece toilet.

In most cases you will be replacing a toilet, not installing one from scratch. So that means you have to remove the old toilet before you can install the new one. If you are installing a toilet in a brand-new area, you can go get a cup of coffee now and skip the old-toilet-removal steps that follow.

But for the rest of you, a word of caution when it comes to removing old toilets. If you have only one toilet in the house, call a licensed plumber to do this job! Why? Because there are a number of things that can go wrong, and if your only toilet is shut down for a day or two while you try to figure things out, needless to say you will have additional problems to deal with besides the original job.

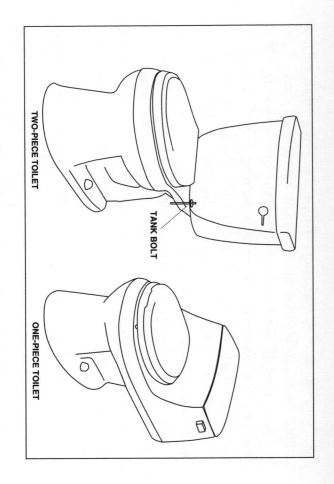

TWO-PIECE TOILET

TANK BOLT

ONE-PIECE TOILET

Tools and Materials Needed: Along with your toilet, toilet seat, hand tools, and safety equipment, you'll need the following specialty tools and materials to install a toilet: a large flathead screwdriver, two adjustable wrenches (one medium-size and one small), needle-nose pliers, small flat hacksaw, force cup plunger, sponge and bucket, plastic paint scraper, drop cloth, and rags. For trim materials needed to install a toilet, make sure you have a closet-bolt kit, flexible braided stainless-steel toilet-supply line, standard wax seal ring, and a deep-seal wax seal ring (if needed for lower toilet flanges).

Removing the Old Toilet

The first step is to make sure the toilet stop or shutoff valve (usually located on the lower-left side of the toilet) is off and holds water. After shutting off the valve, flush the toilet and hold the handle down till all the water drains out of the tank. Now watch the toilet and listen to make sure no water is running past the valve.

Remove the leftover water from the tank and bowl. For the tank, use the big sponge and bucket. For the bowl, push the water out with a plunger, then throw a few old rags into the bowl trap to absorb any remaining water.

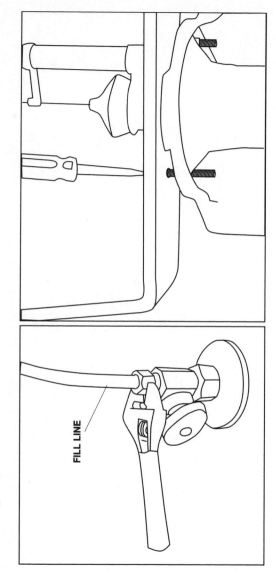

FILL LINE

The old toilet will most likely be a two-piece toilet, and it's a good idea to disconnect the tank from the bowl. First, remove the toilet's water line from the shutoff valve to the tank with your medium adjustable wrench. Also remove the tank-to-bowl nuts and bolts with the large flathead screwdriver and your small adjustable wrench. Once the water line and tank bolts are removed, the tank should lift off the bowl.

The bowl itself is next, and that's connected to the toilet floor flange, usually with two closet bolts. To get access to the closet bolt nuts, pop off the decorative caps with a flathead screwdriver. Then, using the small adjustable wrench, remove the nuts and washers from the closet bolts.

If the entire bolt starts to spin, wedge the flathead screwdriver under the nut washer to hold the bolt still. Once the closet nuts and washers are removed, lift the toilet off the flange and place it on the drop cloth.

If the closet nuts and bolts are rusted in place, hold them with the needle-nose pliers and use the hacksaw to cut the closet bolt just under the nut and washer, just as with the tank bolts. Cutting the bolts will also allow the toilet bowl to be removed from the flange.

Place a rag in the flange drain hole to stop sewer gases and, using the plastic paint scraper, remove the old wax seal. Take out the old closet bolts from the key slots in the flange and inspect the flange for damage. If everything looks good, you can move on. If you have a broken flange, you should contact your plumber.

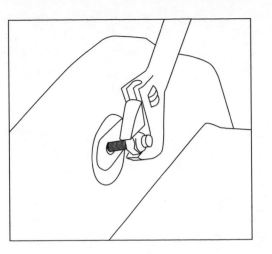

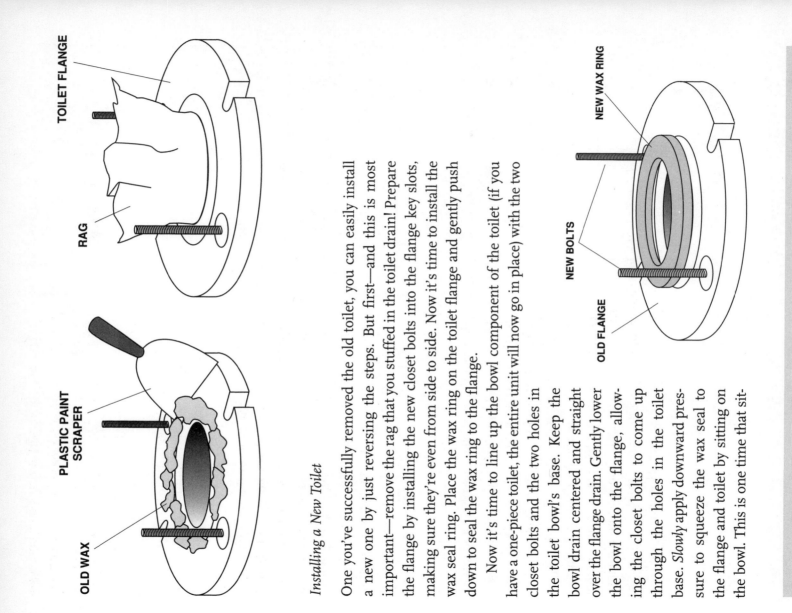

TOILET FLANGE

RAG

PLASTIC PAINT SCRAPER

OLD WAX

NEW WAX RING

NEW BOLTS

OLD FLANGE

Installing a New Toilet

One you've successfully removed the old toilet, you can easily install a new one by just reversing the steps. But first—and this is most important—remove the rag that you stuffed in the toilet drain! Prepare the flange by installing the new closet bolts into the flange key slots, making sure they're even from side to side. Now it's time to install the wax seal ring. Place the wax ring on the toilet flange and gently push down to seal the wax ring to the flange.

Now it's time to line up the bowl component of the toilet (if you have a one-piece toilet, the entire unit will now go in place) with the two closet bolts and the two holes in the toilet bowl's base. Keep the bowl drain centered and straight over the flange drain. Gently lower the bowl onto the flange, allowing the closet bolts to come up through the holes in the toilet base. *Slowly* apply downward pressure to squeeze the wax seal to the flange and toilet by sitting on the bowl. This is one time that sit-

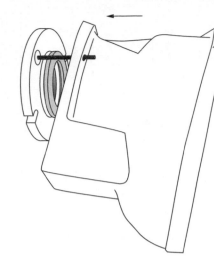

PRO TIP

Most professional plumbers I know, including myself, put the wax ring on the floor flange instead of the toilet discharge hole. It seals the bowl to the flange just as well, and installation is a lot easier! Also, since the ring is in place between the closet bolts, you can pinch a little wax around each bolt to keep them in place when you install the toilet bowl.

ting down on the job is actually the right thing to do!

Install the special cap-locking washers and nuts that come with the toilet onto the closet bolts (be careful not to overtighten) with the small adjustable wrench and gently cut off the excess bolt threads with the hacksaw. Snug up the bolt nuts one more time and snap on the decorative cover caps over each nut.

To mount the tank to the bowl, you need to prep the tank by installing the tank-to-bowl seal ring to the outside bottom of the tank's drain hole. Then place the tank on top of the bowl, lining up the tank drain and gasket to the bowl inlet hole. Next to the tank drain and the bowl inlet are holes for the tank-to-bowl bolts. Place the bolts through the holes, install the nuts and washers, then tighten down the bolts evenly from bolt to bolt (don't overtighten). Some toilets use two tank-to-bowl bolts, and some will use three.

Once the tank is firmly in place and the bowl tightly mounted and sealed to the floor flange, it's time to connect the new water line. Using a flexible braided toilet water-supply line makes this an easy hookup!

Attach and tighten the compression nut of the supply line to the existing shutoff valve for the toilet with the medium adjustable wrench. It's a good idea to support the valve while tightening to avoid stressing it. Then attach the closet connector side of the supply to the tank connection on the toilet. Hand tighten this connection and then snug it up with your medium wrench.

At this point the basic toilet installation is

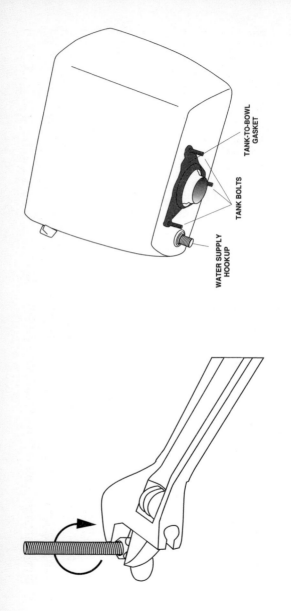

WATER SUPPLY HOOKUP

TANK-TO-BOWL GASKET

TANK BOLTS

complete, and now it's time to test your work. Slowly turn on the water and check for leaks. When the tank is filled to the halfway point, shut down the water. Now you need to test the tank-to-bowl gasket and the floor flange seal by flushing the toilet. This is done with half a tank of water just in case there is a bad leak, so you won't have to clean up a full tank of water!

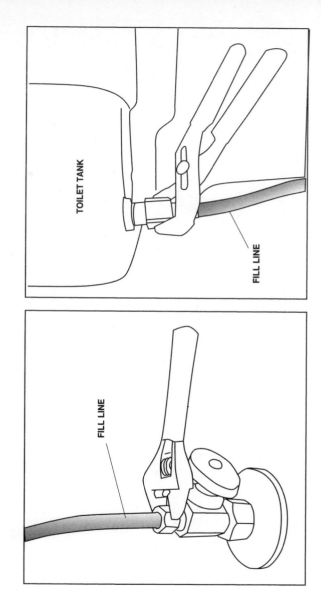

TOILET TANK

FILL LINE

FILL LINE

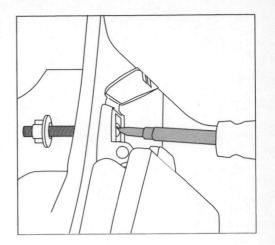

Once you complete all your water-line and seal tests, turn the water back on and fill the tank completely. Make any fill-valve adjustments per your toilet instructions and set the correct water level for your toilet.

Finally, attach the toilet seat. The seat comes with mounting hardware that's basically a nut and bolt for each side of the seat hinge, and the bolts go through the seat holes in the bowl. Hand tighten the nuts from under the bowl and tighten the bolts from the top with the flathead screwdriver.

BATHROOM SINKS AND FAUCETS

In the last few years, projects involving bathroom sinks and faucets have become more specialized. The issue is not complicated plumbing repairs—it goes much deeper than that. Because we live in a society that encourages people to be individuals, the once-basic bathroom faucet and sink combo is long gone. So the big problem we face when trying to learn about bathroom sinks and faucets is that there are too many different types out there!

Lavatory Sinks

Bathroom sinks are referred to as lavatory—or simply lav—sinks by the pros, and that's about the only thing most lav sinks have in common with one another. Styles, shapes, colors, and types of lav sinks cover the full spectrum. Here are a few basic lavatory sink models:

Countertop lavatory: Usually called a "drop-in lav." This is by far the most popular type of bathroom sink. Drop-ins are usually self-rimming and mount directly on top of any vanity top or countertop.

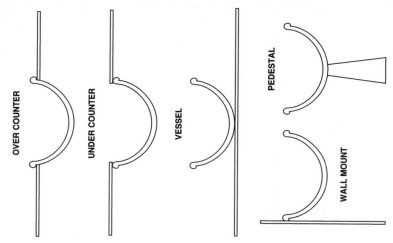

OVER COUNTER

UNDER COUNTER

VESSEL

PEDESTAL

WALL MOUNT

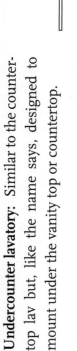

Undercounter lavatory: Similar to the countertop lav but, like the name says, designed to mount under the vanity top or countertop.

Vessel lavatory: Even though most vessel lavs are technically countertop mounts, these high-end sinks are reminiscent of the old china washbasins and look more like decorative bowls resting on a countertop.

Pedestal sink: This type of sink refuses to go away! Pedestal sinks always seem to be in style. They are decorative lav sinks that sit atop matching pedestal bases positioned at a comfortable height.

Wall-mounted lavatory: Often called a "wall-hung" sink, this is a very popular choice for smaller bathrooms. Wall mounting not only saves space but can increase accessibility for special-needs bathrooms.

Faucet Holes in Lav Sinks

There are many variations of the five basic models I just mentioned. Most lav sinks also come precast with faucet holes in place. It's very important you understand the faucet-hole setups for a lav sink so you can get the right faucet to match the right sink.

Depending on the style, lavatory faucets can require one hole or three holes in the sink. But with three-hole lav sinks, the holes are spaced closer together on some models and farther apart on others.

If your faucet requires one hole for installation, the lav sink will need to have one hole on the rim to accept the faucet. This is now referred to as a *one-hole lavatory*. Conversely, if you're changing a faucet

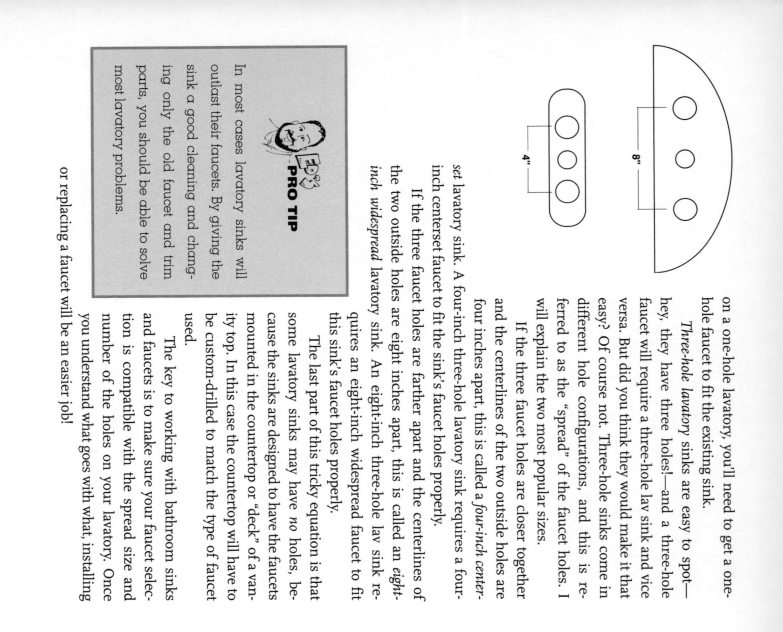

on a one-hole lavatory, you'll need to get a one-hole faucet to fit the existing sink.

Three-hole lavatory sinks are easy to spot—hey, they have three holes!—and a three-hole faucet will require a three-hole lav sink and vice versa. But did you think they would make it that easy? Of course not. Three-hole sinks come in different hole configurations, and this is referred to as the "spread" of the faucet holes. I will explain the two most popular sizes.

If the three faucet holes are closer together and the centerlines of the two outside holes are four inches apart, this is called a *four-inch center-set lavatory sink*. A four-inch three-hole lavatory sink requires a four-inch centerset faucet to fit the sink's faucet holes properly.

If the three faucet holes are farther apart and the centerlines of the two outside holes are eight inches apart, this is called an *eight-inch widespread lavatory sink*. An eight-inch three-hole lav sink requires an eight-inch widespread faucet to fit this sink's faucet holes properly.

The last part of this tricky equation is that some lavatory sinks may have *no* holes, because the sinks are designed to have the faucets mounted in the countertop or "deck" of a vanity top. In this case the countertop will have to be custom-drilled to match the type of faucet used.

The key to working with bathroom sinks and faucets is to make sure your faucet selection is compatible with the spread size and number of the holes on your lavatory. Once you understand what goes with what, installing

PRO TIP

In most cases lavatory sinks will outlast their faucets. By giving the sink a good cleaning and changing only the old faucet and trim parts, you should be able to solve most lavatory problems.

or replacing a faucet will be an easier job!

Quick-Install Faucets

Today there are hundreds of different faucets in use, and each one requires different repair parts and labor techniques in order to complete any faucet-repair job. If your faucet is fairly new and you know the make and model, minor problems should be simple to fix. Just contact the supply house or manufacturer for materials and instructions.

However, take it from my years of experience: When the faucet is older or develops serious problems, in the long run it will usually cost you less money and a lot less aggravation to remove the existing problem faucet and install a new quality faucet so you can start from scratch.

I have seen many homeowners and plumbers chase and order parts for older faucets, and completely disassemble problem faucets and rebuild them, only to have the faucet fail again within a few weeks' time. So now, not only do they have to replace the faucet anyway, but they've lost all the time and money spent trying to repair something old or cheap.

Nowadays installing new faucets is a lot easier than it used to be. While it could have made sense years ago to repair a faucet and avoid all the repiping under the sink, today we have flexible water-supply lines and "quick-install" faucets that install in a snap!

A quick-install faucet is one that's ready to go straight out of the box. The handles and trim parts are preassembled on most models. This not only saves time but also cuts down the chances of losing parts.

Quick-install faucets are called "no-sweat" installations, since in most cases no soldering or repiping of the existing water lines is needed. Flexible water-supply lines are also factory-installed onto the faucet body, with connections that fit most standard shutoff valves under the sink.

Finally, many quick-install faucets have a special expanding mounting, or butterfly, nut that slides in from the top and locks the faucet in place, eliminating the need to tighten up the faucet from underneath the sink. With all these features, it's no wonder that installing a new

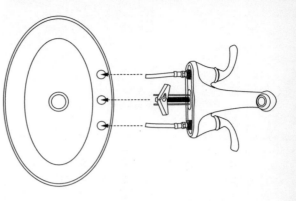

faucet is your best option if you need to make a repair. And upgrading your faucet is an easy way to put a new decorative accent in your bathroom.

The old saying "Out with the old and in with the new" applies perfectly to replacing a lav sink faucet. The sink needs to be stripped of all the old faucet parts before the new faucet can be installed. I recommend that you plan this job knowing that your bathroom sink will be out of use for a good part of the day (maybe longer) and that you'll need to use other sinks in the house while the repairs are being made.

Chances are you're not a plumber working by the hour, so you can slow down and change your faucet step by step. To be sure you do this project correctly, I suggest breaking it up into three separate sections:

1. Demo work—Remove all the old faucet parts and trim.

2. Sizing up—Determine the exact faucet and trim to fit your sink.

3. Finish work—Install the new faucet and trim materials.

This is the trick of all good plumbers and contractors: We never look at a project as one unit. If you break down a job into sections, it becomes easier to manage and reduces the chance of problems.

Removing a Lavatory Faucet

Tools and Materials Needed: Have your complete set of hand tools available, plus large and small pairs of slip-joint pliers, adjustable wrenches, and of course a basin cock wrench.

The very first step when removing the old faucet is to make sure your lav stops (water shutoff valves) located under the sink are working properly and actually shut the water off completely.

Locate the hot and cold lav stops—most standard stops will have

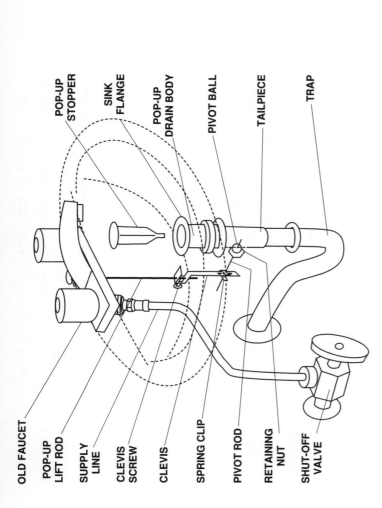

OLD FAUCET
POP-UP LIFT ROD
SUPPLY LINE
CLEVIS SCREW
CLEVIS
SPRING CLIP
PIVOT ROD
RETAINING NUT
SHUT-OFF VALVE

POP-UP STOPPER
SINK FLANGE
POP-UP DRAIN BODY
PIVOT BALL
TAILPIECE
TRAP

chrome "football"-shaped handles. Shut both valves by turning clockwise until you feel them close completely.

To be sure the lav stop valves are holding, turn on the old faucet and look for running water. If any water continues to run through the faucet, tighten up the valves further until all water stops running through the faucet.

When the water is off at the sink, you can now continue the project knowing that if something goes wrong that delays the job, all that will be out of order is the bathroom sink. Every other plumbing fixture in the house can be used as normal. This is called *fixture isolation*, and that's why it's important that stop valves are installed at every fixture.

TROUBLE NOTE

If one or both of the lav stops fail to close and water continues to run through the faucet, it means that you cannot go on with this project until the broken valves can be repaired or replaced.

Back to the faucet removal. Your next step is to disconnect the water lines. Connecting from the lav stop valves to the faucet are small pipes called *supply tubes*. Usually in older homes they'll be made of copper or chrome; on newer installations they can be plastic tubes.

On the stop valves are small compression nuts that can be removed with an adjustable wrench and on the faucet body will be larger compression nuts that you remove with the basin cock wrench. Once you have removed all the compression nuts, pull the supply tubes off the hot and cold faucet connections and stop valves. Completely remove the supply tubes and discard them.

Lavatory faucets have "pop-up" assemblies that work so that when you push down the pop-up rod on the faucet, the drain stop pops up. When you pull the rod up, the drain closes.

Removal of the faucet pop-up assembly is next. Under the sink is a flat rod called a *clevis* that connects to the pop-up rod with a flathead screw called a clevis screw. Remove the flat clevis screw and pull the pop-up rod out from the clevis rod and faucet.

Now slide the clevis rod off the ball rod by removing the spring clip from the ball rod as well, discarding the pop-up rod, clevis, and clip.

The ball rod has a large compression nut that attaches to the pop-up's drain body. Remove the compression nut and ball rod from the drain body and the stopper from the drain body as well, discarding all.

Now the only thing left is to disconnect the drain body and the faucet body from the lav sink. Sounds simple, but this is where the job gets very physical. In some cases, due to frozen or rusted parts, things can get really tough!

The method used to disconnect the drain body depends on its style. Some disconnect from under the sink's drain hole, some from the drain flange on the top inside of the drain hole. All have threaded connections. Most will have a large, flat hex nut with a metal washer and a rubber seal that is loosened from the bottom. Once the nut and seal are loose, the entire assembly can be unscrewed from the sink flange. Remove any debris from the sink's drain hole and clean the drain hole with a rag.

Depending on your trap setup, you may also have to remove the tailpiece from the drain body to completely remove the drain body and tailpiece from the sink and the trap adapter. Discard all.

Last but not least, remove the faucet body from the lav sink. You'll need to get down on your back and get under the sink for this job. Don't forget your basin cock wrench and safety glasses!

Look for the two large, flat faucet-mounting nuts that hold the faucet to the sink. Some faucets have plastic mounting nuts, some have brass nuts, and a few may have smaller mounting nuts with large washers that anchor the faucet to the sink.

Using the basin cock wrench, loosen the nuts by turning them counterclockwise. If they're rusted in place, try some penetrating oil to loosen them up. A helper with a flashlight also makes this job a lot easier.

With the nuts removed, the faucet body can be pulled from the sink holes and discarded. Finally, clean the sink holes with a rag.

Installing a Quick-Install Faucet

As we discussed, you're not restricted to a few faucet choices—you have hundreds and hundreds to choose from! Just remember that once you have your old faucet removed, you need to determine your sink's faucet-hole setup and get a faucet that matches it.

The great thing about quick-install faucets is that they are very universal and should fit all three-hole four-inch centerset lav sinks. Since the majority of bathroom sinks out there are three-hole four-inch centerset sinks, that's what I'll describe how to install.

If you're working with a one-hole sink or a three-hole eight-inch widespread lavatory, you'll have to use a faucet that will fit those sinks. A quick-install faucet exactly like the one we'll be discussing may or may not be available for for every type of sink. Don't worry though—all good faucets include complete and detailed instructions, plus manufacture's help-line numbers. So no matter what type of faucet you need or want for your bathroom sink, just follow "your" instructions!

Tools and Materials Needed: Along with your four-inch centerset quick-install faucet, you'll need an adjustable wrench, a good set of screwdrivers, Teflon paste, and some plumber's putty. If you're installing a more conventional faucet, you'll also need a basin cock wrench.

Installing the Pop-up Assembly: With the sink stripped down and the stop valves and trap under the sink in good working order, you should be ready to go. Remember to give the sink a very good cleaning with a cleaner that will remove rust and water-deposit stains.

In most cases faucets come complete with new pop-up assemblies. No matter what type or style of faucet you install, all pop-up assemblies should install basically the same way.

Apply Teflon paste around the small machine threads of the tailpiece, slide the smooth side of the tailpiece into the trap adapter nut, and hand-tighten the tailpiece and nut onto the trap threads. Make

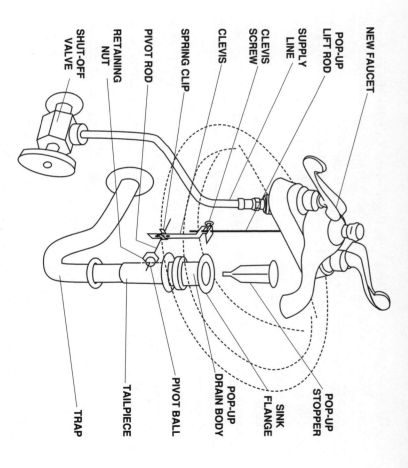

NEW FAUCET

POP-UP
LIFT ROD

SUPPLY
LINE

CLEVIS
SCREW

CLEVIS

SPRING CLIP

PIVOT ROD

RETAINING
NUT

SHUT-OFF
VALVE

POP-UP
STOPPER

SINK
FLANGE

POP-UP
DRAIN BODY

PIVOT BALL

TAILPIECE

TRAP

sure the trap adapter nut is snug enough so the tailpiece does not fall into the trap and loose enough so the tailpiece can be raised and screwed into the pop-up drain body when ready.

Roll out a bead of putty and stick it to the underside of the sink's drain hole flange and press it into the drain hole. The putty should hold the flange temporarily in place.

The pop-up drain body should have the new large hex nut, metal washer, and rubber seal already in place. It's a good idea to apply a little Teflon paste to the rubber seal and machine threads on the drain body.

Push the drain body up through the bottom of the sink hole and carefully thread the drain body onto the sink flange. Have one hand turning the drain body from underneath while you hold the flange in place with your other hand. Once the threads bottom out, stop turning.

Align the pop-up rod hole so it faces the back of the sink. Start turning the flat hex nut with large slip-joint pliers. Keep turning until the washer and seal and flange are compressed tightly to the sink drain. Wipe off any putty and Teflon paste that will squeeze out.

Slide the pop-up stopper inside the drain hole. Put the retaining nut and seals onto the ball rod as per your faucet instructions. Attach the ball rod and nut to the drain body's threads, catching the stopper inside the drain body. Snug up this connection with the rod pointing back. Now slide the tailpiece up into the drain body's threads and tighten the connection firmly. Also tighten the trap adapter.

You should be able to move the rod up and down to test the stopper. The pop-up rod, clevis, and spring clip will be installed once the faucet is in place to complete the pop-up assembly installation.

Installing the Faucet Body: Remember, the following steps are for a quick-install faucet, which is the type I recommend for a standard four-inch centerset lav sink. Many different

PRO TIP

Hooking up the pop-up assembly and drain connection first instead of installing the faucet first will eliminate the possibility of the faucet's running without the drain connected.

makes and models of faucets are available for lav sinks, so follow "your" faucet instructions.

Once you remove the quick-install faucet from the box, it's good to go! The faucet handles, aerator, flexible water lines, rubber deck seal, and mounting bracket are all in place.

Looking down on the sink, you'll see the three faucet holes. The faucet base has a water line on each side and a large butterfly-type nut in the center. With the spout facing you, insert the hot and cold flexible water lines into each outside hole. Then lower the faucet till the center butterfly nut goes through the center hole and locks under the sink.

Pull up on the faucet gently to ensure that the nut has locked into place and the water lines are free and clear. Using the appropriate screwdriver that will fit into the mounting-rod hole at the top of the faucet, start to turn the mounting screw clockwise. Keep turning and you'll notice that the butterfly nut will rise up to the sink rim and lock the faucet in place.

If you're working with a conventional faucet this is where you would have to go under the sink and install the mounting nuts and water supply lines by hand with a basin cock wrench.

With the quick-install faucet body mounted to the sink, the hot and cold water lines can now be connected. At the end of each flexible line will be a compression nut that fits standard stop valves. Attach each nut to the valve threads and tighten with an adjustable wrench.

Now it is time to slide the pop-up rod through the mounting-rod hole. Under the sink attach the clevis to the pop-up rod with the clevis screw. Slide the clevis with the spring clip onto the ball rod. Turn on the water valves and test the faucet operation.

You may need to make adjustments to the pop-up assembly. If you see any drips, tighten the compression nuts.

SHOWERHEADS AND PERSONAL SHOWERS

Few projects around your house are easy to complete and deliver such a useful return on your time and money as changing a showerhead does. This is a project anyone can do, with few skills and tools required. If you've never done a repair project before, here's the one to start with!

Also, because of the wide variety of showerheads and personal showers on the market today, it's almost a guarantee that you'll be thrilled with the results. Water-saving regulations on new high-power showerheads now limit the flow of water to 2.5 gallons a minute per head. However, you can install multiple heads for a custom shower stall or in most cases a standard head with a personal shower setup.

In the past when a showerhead clogged up with water deposits, it was quite common to remove the old head, soak it in a cleaning solution for a day, and then reinstall the same old head! Nowadays people have realized that if you're going to put the effort into removing and reinstalling an old showerhead, it makes more sense to spend a few dollars and install a new water-saving "performance" showerhead at the same time!

In fact, it's a very smart move to change and/or upgrade your present showerhead, even if you've just moved into a new home! In most new homes, the builder will simply install a standard small showerhead to meet minimum requirements. Remember, you set the tone of your day with your morning shower. Why make it a frustrating experience? Go splurge and treat yourself to an exciting power shower!

Replacing a Standard Showerhead

The fun thing about replacing a showerhead is getting to shop for a new-style head that everyone in your family will enjoy! Another good thing is that just about any type of showerhead you choose should be able to be installed on the present chrome shower-arm pipe sticking out of your wall.

Tools and Materials Needed: Along with a new showerhead, you'll need an adjustable wrench, two pairs of slip-joint pliers, and electrical and Teflon tape.

The easy first step when changing a show-

TROUBLE NOTE

Inspect your chrome shower arm before starting this project. A rusted or corroded shower arm can break inside the wall!

erhead is to make sure the water is off going to the showerhead. Since your shower mixing valve supplies the water to the head, there are no isolation valves or main water supplies that need to be located and turned off. If your tub and shower mixing valve is off, your showerhead is off, and you can start the job!

For the first step, you need to do an old plumber's trick called "backing off." Backing off involves using two wrenches to work in opposite directions to keep the pipe and fitting you're disconnecting or installing from spinning in one direction and overstressing other joints in the line. You want to help protect the shower-arm joint inside the wall from loosening up or, worse yet, breaking!

You'll be turning the old showerhead counterclockwise to loosen it, so place the slip-joint pliers on the shower arm in the opposite direction when removing the old head. A little electrical tape wrapped around the jaws of the pliers will help protect any chrome or other finish surfaces from damage.

Removing the Old Showerhead: Size and place the adjustable wrench in the flat slot of the showerhead threaded fitting and back off the

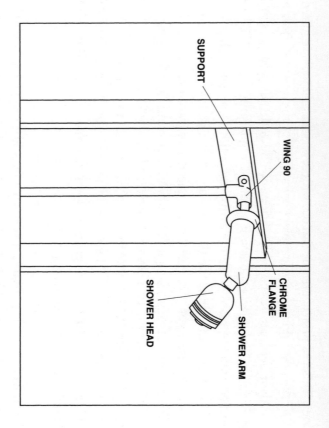

SUPPORT

WING 90

CHROME
FLANGE

SHOWER HEAD

SHOWER ARM

shower arm with the slip-joint pliers. If there is no fitting slot on the showerhead, use the second pair of slip-joint pliers instead to grab the showerhead fitting.

With a good strong grip on both wrenches, slowly loosen the old showerhead's threaded fitting by turning it counterclockwise while holding the shower arm firmly in place with the back-off wrench. Keep turning the showerhead fitting counterclockwise, resetting the wrench or pliers when necessary. Once the showerhead is loose enough to turn by hand, set the tools aside and finish the removal by hand.

Installing the New Showerhead: Make sure the shower arm's threads are clean and free of any old sealants or Teflon tape. Apply a few turns of new Teflon tape clockwise around the threads and snap off the Teflon tape from the roll on the last turn around the threads. The shower arm is now ready to accept a new showerhead.

Prep your new showerhead according to the manufacturer's instructions. Make sure you insert any washers, filter screens, or water restrictors into the showerhead fitting that are required for installation.

With a good hold on the new showerhead, start turning the showerhead's fitting threads by hand onto the shower arm's threads. Hand-tighten the connection as much as possible, before getting the wrenches.

To tighten the showerhead fitting, you'll now be turning the showerhead clockwise to secure it onto the shower arm's threads. So place the back-off wrench or slip-joint pliers on the shower arm in the opposite direction from when you removed the head.

With the shower arm firmly supported by the back-off wrench, continue to tighten the showerhead fitting clockwise, using the second adjustable wrench or pliers to turn the showerhead fitting.

Just as for the removal, reset the showerhead fitting wrench when necessary while keeping the back-off wrench on the shower arm locked in place to prevent the shower arm from spinning.

PRO TIP

Be sure to reverse the direction of the back-off wrench when installing the new showerhead!

Once the head fitting is tightened up on to the shower arm, remove any excess strands of Teflon tape and clean the shower arm and showerhead with a rag. Point the showerhead into the tub and turn on your tub and shower mixing valve to test your new showerhead!

If you notice any drips or leaks from the showerhead fitting, in most cases it's a simple job to tighten the fitting up a little more till the dripping stops. Remember, it's better to snug up a showerhead fitting till the dripping stops, than to overtighten the fitting during installation and possibly crack the showerhead fitting or damage the shower arm.

Installing a Standard Personal Shower

A personal shower is a great addition to any tub or shower stall. Basically, a personal shower is a showerhead on an extension hose, giving the user greater flexibility to reach—how shall we say—"personal" places with the shower water. Also, a personal shower is very convenient for washing pets or whenever you need to keep water from splashing outside the tub and shower surround.

There are two basic styles of personal-shower kits. First, there are lower-end standard models that attach directly to the shower arm. This type has a locking bracket built into the shower-arm connection to hold one spray head and the extension hose. There are also high-end customized personal-shower kits. This type uses a diverter valve with one standard showerhead and a second remote spray head with a hose that mounts on a sliding wall bracket.

Just as with most home-improvement decisions, determining which type of personal shower you choose for your tub and shower surround will depend on your budget and/or the work involved for the results you want. Lower-priced units that mount on the shower arm install in minutes, while the higher-priced wall-mounted kits require some time to complete the job.

Shower-Arm Mount: The great thing about arm-mounted personal showers is that they are as easy to install as a new standard showerhead. The special connection fitting to the shower arm has a built-in bracket that holds the hose and personal shower in place when not in use and allows the personal shower to be used like a standard shower-head.

Tools and Materials Needed: Along with an arm-mounted personal shower kit, you'll need two slip-joint pliers and both electrical and Teflon tape.

Wrap the teeth of the pliers with electrical tape to avoid any scratching while you back off and remove the old showerhead, as explained earlier. With the head removed, follow your kit's installation instructions. In most cases you'll apply Teflon tape to the shower arm's threads and then install the personal shower's fitting bracket to the shower arm's threads as you would a new showerhead. Don't forget to once again back off.

After the fitting bracket is mounted, it's time to attach the hose and spray head. The fitting bracket should have a threaded connection for the personal shower hose at the bottom, pointing toward the base of the tub or shower.

Place the rubber washers provided with the kit into both the shower-hose fittings and connect one of the hose fittings to the bracket's threaded connection with the slip-joint pliers. Since it's a washer-type fitting, in most cases Teflon tape will not be needed.

The spray head also has a threaded connection that attaches to the second hose fitting the same way. Make sure all your connections are snug but not overtightened. Many arm-mounted units are made with plastic and can easily be damaged if the fittings are stressed.

Snap or slide the personal showerhead into the shower-arm bracket, make any necessary adjustments, and point the shower in the direction you want. Hand-tighten the bracket's adjustment ring to lock the bracket in place, in order to keep the showerhead in position. Finally, turn on the water to test out your new personal shower!

Personal Shower with Diverter and Slide Bar

The big feature with the upgraded wall-mount kit is a vertically mounted chrome bar with a sliding bracket that allows the personal shower to be used as a showerhead you can set for different heights. With this type of kit, children and adults of all sizes can enjoy a custom shower!

Also included in the kit is a diverter valve. This is a directional switch for water that can divert the water in one direction or the other. Some diverters can also divert the water in two directions at once. Standard diverters have two connection outlets, one for a fixed showerhead and one for the personal shower, giving you a two-for-one deal!

Tools and Materials Needed: Along with a wall-mounted personal shower kit, you'll need a screwdriver set, two-foot level, power drill and bits, two slip-joint pliers, stud finder, caulking, and electrical and Teflon tape.

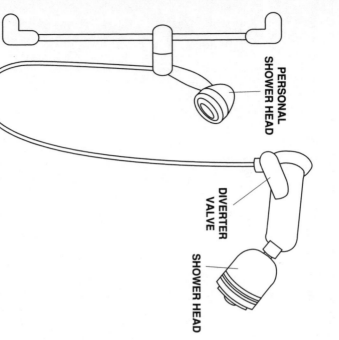

PERSONAL SHOWER HEAD

DIVERTER VALVE

SHOWER HEAD

Once again wrap the teeth of the pliers with electrical tape to avoid any scratching while you remove the old showerhead, as explained earlier. With the head removed, follow your kit's installation instructions. Usually you'll first install the diverter valve onto the shower arm's threads as you would a new showerhead. Don't forget to use Teflon tape on the shower arm's threads and back off as usual.

When the diverter is installed, you can now reinstall the original showerhead onto the diverter showerhead onto the diverter threads, pointing straight out, or install a new showerhead onto the diverter as you would any showerhead. This time, however, make sure you back off on the diverter and showerhead with the wrenches.

Now it's time to mount the vertical sliding bar for the shower. Keep in mind that this vertical bar is *not* designed to be a shower grab bar. It's designed to change the height of the personal shower and hold it in place. Make sure you follow the mounting instructions and be careful not to place the bar in an area where water lines could be located.

In most cases the water lines for the mixing valve and showerhead will run up the middle of the front wall of the tub and shower unit. To avoid the likely spot of the water lines, it's recommended that you offset the vertical bar to the right or left of the mixing valve at least enough to miss the water lines.

Once you find a good place for the bar, use the stud finder to locate and mark the nearest wall stud. With the two-foot level, draw a vertical line longer than the length of the bar. Hold the bar over the line and mark the holes for the wall flanges on the bar.

With the proper size and type of bit, drill out the holes at the flange marks. Stop as soon as you penetrate the tub and shower surround, and this should prevent the drill from going deep into the stud or wall pocket.

If you've located a stud, the stainless-steel screws provided with the kit will be able to go directly into the stud. If you miss the stud on some of the holes, you'll need to use the plastic wall-shield anchors that come with the kit to secure the bar to the wall.

Insert the plastic wall shields into any of the hollow holes not located over a wall stud and apply a small dab of caulking to every hole you've drilled, including those over the stud.

Place the bar and flanges over the appropriate holes and screw the bar to the wall with the stainless-steel screws. Do not tighten the screws completely until all the screws have been started.

With the vertical bar mounted securely to the wall, the last step is to connect the personal shower's hose with the washers to the second threaded outlet on the diverter valve and the connection to the spray head itself.

PRO TIP

To properly drill the holes, you need the right bit for the job. A fiberglass tub and shower surround can be drilled with standard high-speed bits, while a tile wall has to be drilled with a special tile or masonry bit. Also, with a tile wall, try to drill on the grout lines whenever possible to cut down the chances of the bit's traveling or cracking through a tile.

Place the spray head and hose onto the sliding bracket located on the vertical bar. Adjust the height and direction of the spray head and turn on the shower mixing valve. Once the standard showerhead starts to run, push or turn on the diverter valve to test the personal shower.

TUB AND SHOWER GRAB BARS

For decades, tub and shower grab bars have been associated with special-needs bathrooms and were virtually nonexistent in standard residential bathrooms. Bathroom grab bars were also very "hospital-looking" and plain, usually just a bare, curved stainless-steel tube with the anchoring lag screws in plain view. Thanks to the Baby Boomers, things are changing!

Now that a large percentage of the population is getting on in years, the benefit of shower grab bars has finally started to catch on in the home-building industry. With the current residential demand and interest for grab bars in our tubs and showers, the manufacturers have also caught on. Decorative grab bars with many attractive features and finishes are now available to homeowners. The great thing about this project is that just about any existing tub and shower unit can be adapted to accept a new grab-bar kit.

Style and Location

As I mentioned, grab bars are no longer just bent pieces of bare stainless-steel tubing. The good news is that grab bars are now available in many sizes, shapes, and styles to match just about any bathroom. The bad news is, this now means your "first" step will be doing some product research and measuring of your

TROUBLE NOTE

Grab-bar installation is very serious business! Your safety will depend on the grab bar's being properly installed and anchored directly into the wall studs with lag screws. Improperly hung grab bars can actually be a bigger hazard than none at all! Also, consult your building inspector for local hanging regulations.

tub and shower surround to order the grab bar that will best fit your tub and match your present fixtures.

Once you have the grab bar, it's time to find the best place in your tub and shower surround to hang the bar. Keep these three hanging guidelines in mind to avoid problems:

1. *Ease of reach*—Make sure that everyone in your family has easy access to the bar and will be able to reach it and get a good firm grip. Keep in mind that children will grow, so getting a longer bar that you can hang vertically will compensate for any changes in user height along the way.

2. *Avoid hazards*—You will be drilling into the walls of the tub and shower surround. Take precautions and choose locations away from wires, ducts, and piping that may be inside the walls. For instance, the front wall of a tub and shower unit is called the "wet wall" because it has the mixing valve and water lines running up its middle section. Hanging the bar to the far left or right side on this wall will usually avoid the water lines.

3. *Proper backing*—The goal is to have a grab bar that will be almost as strong as the wall itself. Whether you anchor directly into the wall studs or install heavy plywood backing behind the open pockets of the wall, the grab bar's lag screws or bolts will need solid materials to bite into. Don't rely on plastic shields or expanding sleeves mounted in hollow, thin walls. If necessary, you may have to open up the back side of the shower wall to install additional backing or have extra backing built into new tub and shower surrounds.

Installing the Grab Bar

With all the prep work done, you can now hang the bar, following the instructions and using the hardware that comes with the grab

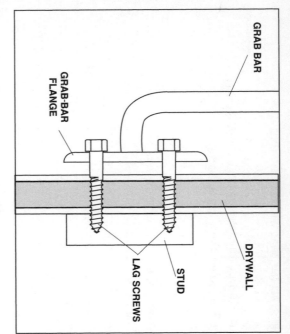

bar. If your grab bar does not come with a mounting kit and you need to buy your own mounting hardware, make sure the lag screws and washers are rated for the size grab bar you have. Also, keep in mind that a shower is a very wet place, so stainless-steel lag screws, bolts, and washers are required.

Tools and Materials Needed: Along with your grab bar and safety equipment, you'll need your hand tools, ratchet set, electronic stud finder, drill with tile bit (for a tile wall) and/or standard bits, a good level, caulking, and the complete mounting hardware package for the grab bar.

Vertical Installation: The advantages with a vertical-mounting grab bar are that you only have to locate one stud and the length of the bar can vary, because the stud also goes up and down vertically. Unless you have additional wall backing, make sure you get a grab bar with the correct flange holes for a vertical mount on one stud. Also, since the bar hangs vertically, get a finish that has a good hand-gripping surface.

Measure and locate the area where you want to hang the bar. Comb the area with a quality electronic stud finder, double-checking that you have located the desired stud. If possible, also check from the back side of the tub/shower wall as well to confirm. A good stud finder will even locate the edges of the wall stud, so outline the stud's edge locations. Line up and level the bar and place the top and bottom flange holes over the center of the stud, then trace the holes to mark where you need to drill into the wall.

Drill through all the marked holes with the proper bit for your tub/shower wall until you hit the wall stud. Aside from using a tile or standard drill bit for your type of shower wall, also make sure it's the correct size for your mounting hardware.

Apply caulking to the back side of the bar flanges and the mounting holes in the wall. Now line up the flanges with the holes and install the lags. Don't tighten the lag screws down until all the lags have been started into the holes. Once all the lags are started, firmly tighten the lag screws into place with the ratchet until the bar has no movement at all. Wipe off the excess caulking and your vertical grab bar is installed!

Horizontal Installation: Horizontal bars will provide you with a wider area to grab than a vertical bar. The process for finding and marking the wall studs is the same as for the vertical installation, but remember that since a horizontal grab bar goes from side to side, you will have to locate two wall studs, one for each side of the bar flanges.

A horizontal hang can be a little tricky. Wall studs are built sixteen inches on center, so you need a horizontal bar with the hanging flanges set for sixteen inches on center. In some horizontal installations, additional behind-the-wall backing may have to be added to make the horizontal installation a little more forgiving and allow for longer grab-bar lengths.

Once you locate the studs or backing, level and mark the bar and the flange holes. With all your proper markings on the wall, drill, hang, caulk, and lag the bar into place just as in the vertical installation.

Offset Installation: As I mentioned, horizontal installations can be a little tricky unless additional backing is installed. But as an alternative, there is a method of installing grab bars from side to side that makes it easier to hang the bar between two studs with little need for additional backing.

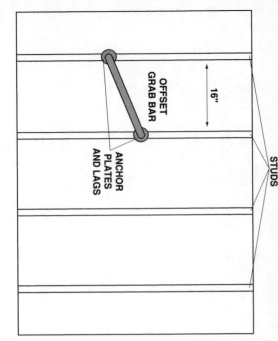

This type of installation is called an *offset* or a diagonal installation. It's a very simple installation that will work and in most cases allow the grab bar's flanges to anchor directly into two wall studs. The trick is to get a grab bar longer than the sixteen-inch difference between studs. A two-foot bar is ideal for an offset installation, but varying sizes can be used.

Just as with the vertical and horizontal installations, the most important step here is to properly mark the stud locations and to use two studs no more than sixteen inches apart. Obviously, the edges of a two-foot bar will not hit both studs if it's hung horizontally. The trick is to place one side of the bar flange directly on one of the stud markings and position the bar straight out past the second stud. Now angle the bar back inward on a diagonal until you hit dead center of the second stud.

You will have to consider height as well as side-to-side location. Also, the grab bar's flange holes are usually three to a flange, set up in a triangular manor. This type of flange hole arrangement should ensure that at least two holes will line up directly with the center of the stud.

Once the flange holes are marked, drill, hang, caulk, and lag the bar into the studs as in the previous installations. Always anchor grab bars to the wall according to the manufacturer's recommendations.

BATHROOM EXHAUST FANS

The old expression "in with the good air, out with the bad air" applies when you're trying to save someone's life. Unfortunately, some people don't understand how important this concept is when it comes to the life of their bathroom. With all those plumbing fixtures packed into a small space, most bathrooms will inevitably become very moist areas. To my dismay, many homeowners and their family members never use the exhaust fan for their bathroom unless it's wired directly in with the light switch.

I bet some of you believe that you are using your exhaust fans properly and think the fan is just meant for eliminating bathroom odors when company is over. While your bathroom fan does help to control normal odors, the real reason for an exhaust fan in your bathroom is to control the moisture. Odors, although embarrassing, will not normally damage your bathroom. Moisture, on the other hand, can cause a lot of problems for any bathroom!

Fresh-air intake for a bathroom is key to avoiding moisture-related problems like mold, mildew, and material damage. Ideally, you should use the fan every time you enter your bathroom and leave it on for at least twenty minutes after you use any fixture. Now—and be honest— how many of you are actually using your exhaust fan properly?

Once you realize the importance of good bathroom ventilation, the first bathroom project you should take on is to inspect all the components of your exhaust system for proper operation and address any necessary repairs.

Fan Maintenance

Because of changes to most building codes years ago that required bathroom ventilation, chances are you will already have an exhaust fan installed in your bathroom. In some older homes, you may find bathrooms that have no exhaust fan at all. Back then the best way to ventilate the bathroom was simply to open the window. That's why there were a lot of windows actually built inside the tub and shower surrounds!

When dealing with an older bathroom with no exhaust system, you need to consult your building inspector or a licensed contractor to determine if it's possible to install a fan into the existing ceiling and walls and if the older electrical wiring can be used without any major renovations.

If you have a bathroom exhaust fan, you can inspect it and the system yourself to determine if it's working properly and if your bathroom is getting the recommended ventilation. Any problems you find will need to be addressed, and the good news is that in most cases, with existing bathroom fans in place, the repairs can be done easily.

Locate and follow the manufacturer's instructions for working with your unit—this could be the hardest part of the job! Luckily, most exhaust fans are designed to be easily serviced and maintained by the homeowner. Regular maintenance will include changing the lightbulb, cleaning the internal parts of the unit, and possibly changing the fan motor if it ever fails. Plus, your room needs to be properly vented to provide a good flow of fresh air in and out of the bathroom.

Tools and Materials Needed: Only hand tools and a small ladder are needed for the maintenance projects that follow.

Changing the Fan Lightbulb

If your fan has a built-in light, you will have to change a blown bulb from time to time. I have seen many families use the fan without a light for years because they were unsure of how to remove the fan cover. By the way, removing the cover is the only tricky part. Once the cover is off, if you can change a lightbulb, you can complete this job! Also, when you learn how to remove your fan's cover, all the other related maintenance jobs will be a lot easier!

Removing the Fan Cover: Use a sturdy stepladder and wear safety glasses. First, turn off the power. Once the cover comes off, chances are there will be debris like bugs and critters trapped in the cover or inside the fan unit. The last thing you want is to be startled on the ladder if stuff falls onto you, so be prepared for this. Locate any screws that may be recessed in the cover and remove them. In some cases, once the screws or nuts are loosened, you may have to turn the cover counterclockwise to remove it.

Some covers can simply snap off to expose internal screws, while many common covers are held in place by V-shaped metal springs that are exposed when you gently pull down the cover. Once the springs are exposed, squeeze the ends of the V together, and if you pull the springs out of the slots, it will give you clear access inside the fan housing.

Cleaning the Fan and Housing

A blown lightbulb is a good opportunity to clean the fan as well as change the bulb. You don't need to schedule cleaning; simply clean the unit at each bulb changing. Once the cover is off and the old bulb is removed, you now have access to vacuum out any dust and debris. Since bathrooms are moist places, look for any rust or corrosion. A small, stiff brass brush is great for removing rust. Also, inspect the fan to make sure it spins freely.

Changing the Fan Motor

If your motor does not spin freely, makes loud noises, or does not run at all, chances are you need a new fan motor. Once you remove the cover, the lightbulb, and in some units the lightbulb bracket as well, you should now have clear access to the motor itself. You should also see a make and model label inside the housing or on the motor, listing all the specifications you need to know for ordering a new fan from the manufacturer.

PRO TIP

When changing a fan motor, remember that the job is not an emergency! Don't start it until you get the new fan motor, and then follow the instructions that come with the new motor. Most fan motors actually plug in to an electrical outlet in the housing, so there's no complicated electrical work! As long as you get the right part, the old motor can be removed and the new motor installed in minutes!

Fan Airflow

If you're inspecting your bathroom's present ventilating system or installing a new vent system from scratch, there are some guidelines you need to follow to ensure proper ventilation. Think of your venting system as a chain. If one of the links does not do its job, the entire system will fail. The three main links in the venting chain are:

- Adequate fresh-air intake.

- Proper exhaust venting.

- Appropriate motor size.

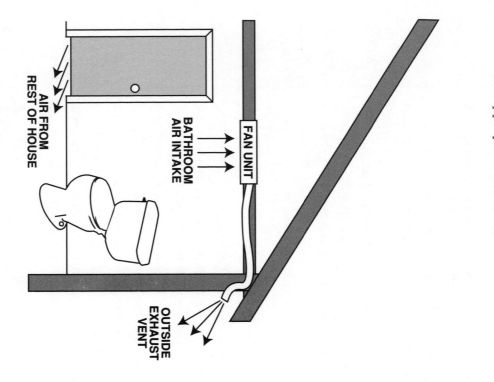

AIR FROM
REST OF HOUSE

BATHROOM
AIR INTAKE

FAN UNIT

OUTSIDE
EXHAUST
VENT

Intake: To move moist air out, you must have an intake opening to get the fresh air in. Bathrooms usually have one entrance, and the fresh-air intake will usually come from the normal half-inch gap under the bathroom door. If your bathroom door does not have an adequate gap or an intake vent to allow fresh air to enter, then chances are you're not moving enough air through your bathroom! *Solution:* Trim the bottom of the bathroom door to create at least half-inch gap, or install a new door with a built-in intake vent.

Exhaust: The size and length of the exhaust duct will depend on the fan unit's specifications, and the duct should have smooth internal surfaces with few bends for the best airflow. The duct has to be vented to the outside with a dryer-type hood and flap to prevent backdrafts. Check to make sure that your bathroom fan does not exhaust directly into the attic. Venting into the attic can cause moisture problems throughout your home, and if this situation exists, it needs to be corrected. *Solution:* Extend the exhaust duct through the roof or an outside wall with an external venting kit.

Sizing: Check to see if your fan motor is the right size for your bathroom. Fans are rated for CFMs (cubic feet per minute), and the bathroom's size will determine the fan's CFM rating. For instance, an eight-by-eight-foot bathroom should use a fan rated around 102 CFMs to supply the recommended twelve air changes an hour. *Solution:* Use a standard formula for getting the total air volume of a bathroom (length times width times height), and divide the air volume by five to get the needed CFMs. If your current fan motor's CFMs are too small, you should upgrade your fan to a larger size for proper ventilation.

We've come a long way from the simple outhouse. Today's bathrooms are very complex and complicated rooms. Future technology will take us even further away from the bathroom's humble beginnings, and soon you'll be seeing computers running our bathrooms!

From whirlpools that can be filled and turned on by cell phone calls on your way home from work, to voice-activated HDTV screens built into our shaving and makeup mirrors, the bathroom will continue to be a room fit for a king. Let's not forget that every king does need a throne, and of course your bathroom will always have that as well.

KITCHEN PROJECTS

GARBAGE DISPOSERS 117

Resetting a garbage disposer breaker overload 117

Garbage disposer maintenance and clogs 118

FAUCETS 120

Installing a new kitchen faucet 121

SINKS AND COUNTERTOPS 130

Replacing a standard kitchen sink 132

Types of countertops 138

REFRIGERATOR DISPENSERS 139

Making the tap 140

Installing the tap-in tee 141

Refrigerator piping choices 143

Running the supply line 144

Refrigerator and water connections 145

Final tips and tricks with ice makers 148

REPLACING A DISHWASHER 149

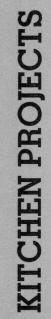

Ed's words of wisdom on kitchens: *Today's kitchens have the perfect in-gredients to become the heart and soul of any home.*

The kitchen has become the new living and entertainment area for many homes. From under-cabinet LCD TVs and custom lighting to built-in sound systems and even high-speed Internet access, in some homes the kitchen is the main room for guests and families to meet and greet.

Gone are the days when one person had to cook in a small pantry while everyone else gathered in the living and dining rooms entertaining one another and waiting for the meal to be prepared.

Today it's common practice for the entire group to be involved in preparing the meal together in a large kitchen area. Also, because kitchens are now set up to be such fun and comfortable work spaces, the entertainment is creating the meal!

Since kitchens are used so often by so many people, the wear and tear on appliances, faucets, and fixtures has also drastically increased.

Plus, since there are so many gadgets you can put into a kitchen, you now have a greater chance for kitchen components to fail.

If you don't understand the basic operation of your major kitchen components and how to handle common kitchen problems and emergencies, your next party could fail as well!

GARBAGE DISPOSERS

One of the most overworked appliances in a kitchen is the garbage disposer. It's also one of the most mispronounced appliances in the kitchen. I have heard them called "disposals," "disposes," even "disposealls," but you may not know that the professional term is "disposer"!

Aside from all the name confusion, a garbage disposer is in fact a sensitive kitchen appliance that needs electrical breaker protection. If a disposer jams up, that means the motor has stopped turning. If the motor stops spinning with the electrical switch in the "on" position, the electricity powering the motor could cause the motor to overheat and burn out.

To avoid this hazardous situation, disposers have built-in power breaker switches. Many homeowners have no idea that breaker switches even exist in garbage disposers, and they'll call a service technician for a fix that can be done with the push of a button.

Resetting a Garbage Disposer Breaker Overload

To reset a disposer breaker, first confirm that the breaker has tripped. Look underneath the disposer and on most disposers you'll see a little square red button off to one side. Usually the button will be recessed, but if you see that the button has popped up out of the housing, that's a definite sign the disposer has tripped its electrical breaker. Check your manual for the location and tripped position of your breaker.

Next, make sure the electricity is completely off to the disposer itself by turning off the power switch and the circuit breaker for the unit at the main panel. Then make sure any debris that has jammed up the

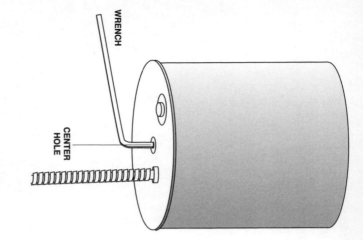

RESETTING BUTTON

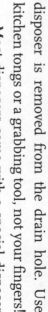

WRENCH

CENTER HOLE

disposer is removed from the drain hole. Use kitchen tongs or a grabbing tool, not your fingers!

Most disposers come with a special disposer wrench that allows you to turn the motor from a center hole under the unit. This should allow you to free the stuck grinder disk by inserting the wrench and moving the wrench back and forth.

Once the wrench spins freely, remove it and press the reset button till it snaps back into place. Turn on the panel circuit breaker, then the switch to start the disposer. If the breaker pops again or the unit buzzes or fails to start, shut it down and call a technician. But in most cases it will go back to normal operation.

Garbage Disposer Maintenance and Clogs

Most standard kitchen sinks are set up with just the one-trap, double-bowl drain system. But many homes also have the addition of a garbage disposer on the kitchen drain lines. If you have a garbage disposer in your kitchen sink, you need to follow some care tips to help prevent sink clogs and ensure proper operation of your disposer.

If the breaker on your disposer overloads and shuts down the motor, reset it and restart the unit as per the instructions I gave you in the disposer breaker overload section. For all other disposer maintenance issues, just follow these tips for disposer care:

- Always run a strong, cold stream of water twenty seconds before grinding food waste and at least twenty seconds after grinding.

- Don't grind food waste using hot water. Hot water may expand the grinding mechanism and strain the unit. However, it is all right to drain hot water through the disposer when it's not in use.

- Don't ever pour food grease into your disposer or drains! Acceptable amounts of hard materials such as chicken bones, fruit pits, and coffee grounds are okay.

- Do not grind fibrous and stringy materials like celery, broccoli, and corn husks in a disposer.

- To cut down odors in a disposer, grind up a lemon once a month or when needed.

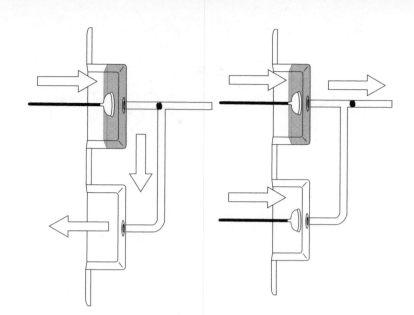

Kitchen Sink Clogs: No matter how careful you are, a kitchen clog may still happen. My pro tip to clear a kitchen sink clog in a double bowl sink is to use two force cup plungers. Place one plunger in each sink drain hole and use my standard plunger technique of slowly pushing down and then sharply pulling up. With two plungers working, this will create double suction on the drain line and should clear most common kitchen sink clogs. Plunging one bowl without blocking the other bowl gives the pressure a place to escape.

FAUCETS

Today's kitchens may be the centerpiece of most homes, but it's the kitchen faucet that's considered the centerpiece of most kitchens. In my years as a contractor, I've seen kitchen faucets evolve from basic on/off valves for delivering water to a sink into beautiful pieces of artwork that can turn themselves on and off automatically with electrical sensors!

With all the attention given to kitchen faucets, there's no excuse for not repairing or upgrading your present faucet. I've gone into a lot of houses that have had nice kitchens, but once I got a good look at the dingy faucet with a broken spray head or duct tape wrapped on the spout, the entire kitchen lost its appeal to me. It's not only cosmetic—who wants to wake up every morning and fill a coffeepot with a faucet that works more like a lawn sprinkler than a pot filler!

A good-quality kitchen faucet can last a lifetime. My major piece of advice to you about the kitchen is to think about upgrading to a new type of faucet that will better match your lifestyle and kitchen. It will be money well spent! Here are the types of kitchen faucets to choose from, each one of which comes in a variety of finishes and styles:

ONE-HANDLE FAUCET

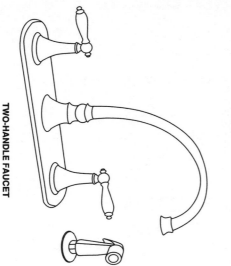

TWO-HANDLE FAUCET

Two-Handle: This is the style of kitchen faucet that would match a more traditional kitchen. A great advantage to two-handle kitchen faucets is that many styles have high-arched "gooseneck" spouts that are both attractive and convenient for filling large containers and pots. The disadvantage is that you need to use two hands for controlling and setting the water temperature.

PULL-OUT SPRAY HEAD

One-Handle: The big advantage here is that the one handle controls both the hot and cold water. One-handle designs offer a better mix and easier operation than the traditional two-handle faucets. While you can find one-handle designs with gooseneck spouts, the majority have lower-angled spouts because the handle sits atop the faucet.

Pullout Spray: These are usually one-handle faucets that feature a pull-out spray head and hose at the end of the spout. Pullout spray faucets offer great mobility and eliminate the need for a remote spray head on the sink deck. A typical pullout spray faucet will usually require only three sink holes, which frees up the fourth sink hole for the installation of other accessories, like a soap dispenser.

Installing a New Kitchen Faucet

If your present kitchen sink faucet is old and not working properly or if it's leaking, in most cases it will make more sense to replace the entire kitchen faucet than to repair it. This will eliminate the hassle of tracking down the correct parts, taking the old faucet apart, installing the new parts, and then trying to put everything back together again without having it squirt you in the face!

Best-case scenario, you successfully repair your old faucet and what do you get for all your time and effort? The same dingy-looking, out-of-date faucet that you started off with. If you're going to put time

PRO TIP

To replace a standard kitchen faucet, there's usually no need to change the basket drain assembly. This eliminates any extra drain work, and that's why it's usually an easier fix to replace an old kitchen faucet instead of repairing one. Unlike bathroom faucets, kitchen faucets do not use pop-up assemblies, and most kitchen faucets come with only the faucet and trim, with no drain fittings.

and money into a project, you should at least end up with a nice new look for your kitchen!

Tools and Materials Needed—Once you choose your type of kitchen faucet and spray, you'll also need flexible water-supply tubes (if your faucet does not come with the supply lines), plumber's putty, Teflon tape, and rags. Along with your hand tool kit and safety glasses, make sure you have two adjustable wrenches and your basin cock wrench.

The first step here, as with most plumbing projects, is to properly shut off the water valves at the fixture. Kitchen sinks will usually have standard water-supply stop valves located under the sink. Turn off the hot and cold valves and open the faucet to make sure the water is off.

Once the water is confirmed off to the kitchen faucet, you can remove the supply tubes between the stop valves and the faucet. These are usually three-eighths-inch water lines with three-eighths-inch compression fittings on the stop valves and half-inch compression fittings at the hot and cold faucet connections. One-handle kitchen faucets may have three-eighths-inch connections on both ends or connect with built-in supply tubes directly to the stop valves.

Use your adjustable wrenches to disconnect the supply-line compression fittings from the stops, making sure you back off the valves to prevent straining the water lines. Use the basin cock wrench to reach up under the sink to disconnect the larger faucet compression fittings.

Rags and safety glasses are a must, because debris and water may rain down on you, so be ready for it! When the compression fittings are disconnected you should be able to work out the copper or flexible tubing from the fitting housings. Once the supply lines are removed, the faucet is now disconnected from the main plumbing system.

Now it's time to remove the kitchen

TROUBLE NOTE

Some old kitchen sink installations may have hard-soldered copper valves, piping, and joints connecting directly to the kitchen faucet. This will prevent you from doing a standard faucet change-out, and a licensed plumber should be consulted.

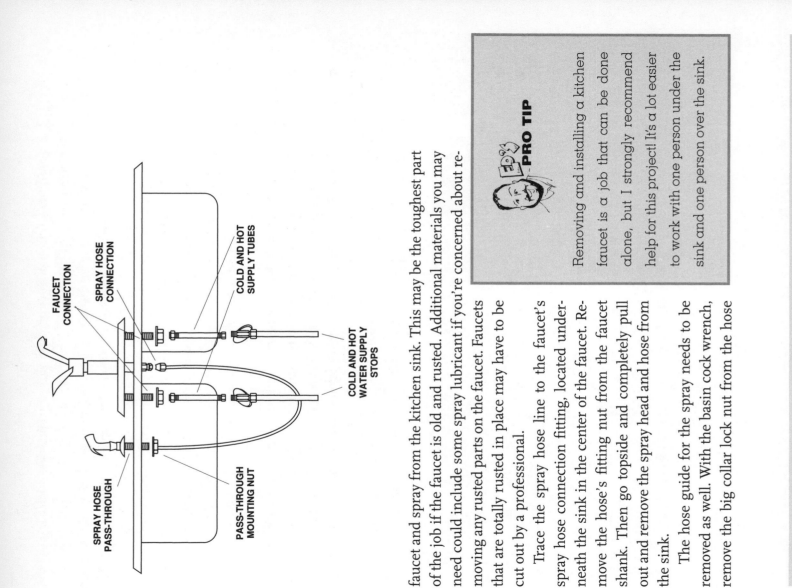

FAUCET CONNECTION

SPRAY HOSE CONNECTION

SPRAY HOSE PASS-THROUGH

PASS-THROUGH MOUNTING NUT

COLD AND HOT SUPPLY TUBES

COLD AND HOT WATER SUPPLY STOPS

faucet and spray from the kitchen sink. This may be the toughest part of the job if the faucet is old and rusted. Additional materials you may need could include some spray lubricant if you're concerned about removing any rusted parts on the faucet. Faucets that are totally rusted in place may have to be cut out by a professional.

Trace the spray hose line to the faucet's spray hose connection fitting, located underneath the sink in the center of the faucet. Remove the hose's fitting nut from the faucet shank. Then go topside and completely pull out and remove the spray head and hose from the sink.

The hose guide for the spray needs to be removed as well. With the basin cock wrench, remove the big collar lock nut from the hose

PRO TIP

Removing and installing a kitchen faucet is a job that can be done alone, but I strongly recommend help for this project! It's a lot easier to work with one person under the sink and one person over the sink.

Kitchen Projects • 123

pass-through under the sink and pull the chrome finish ring off the sink top.

Once you remove the spray, hose, and hose guide from the kitchen sink, it's time to remove the old faucet. Most kitchen faucets are called "deck-mounted" faucets. Deck mounting means that the faucet is one complete unit tied to a deck plate that covers three sink holes.

The deck of a kitchen faucet is held in place with two large mounting nuts on each end of the mounting plate. One-handle faucets usually have built-in supply tubes in the middle hole, along with the spray connection and threaded bolts for each end hole to anchor the mounting nuts.

On two-handle kitchen faucets, only the spray connection is in the middle hole, and the mounting fittings on the end holes do double duty. The outer fitting threads hold the mounting nuts in place as well as secure the compression fittings for the water-supply tubes.

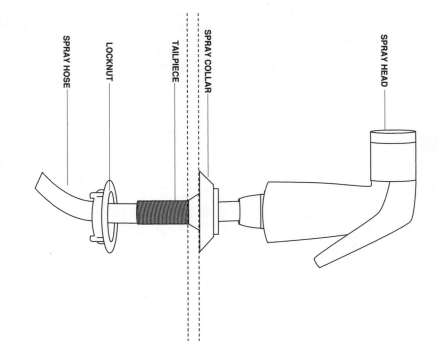

SPRAY HOSE

LOCKNUT

TAILPIECE

SPRAY COLLAR

SPRAY HEAD

At this point the water-supply tubes and fittings will be disconnected, so you can now use your basin cock wrench to loosen and remove the mounting nuts from the faucet's mounting threads. The large mounting nuts should turn counterclockwise off the threads. Plastic nuts come off pretty easily, but older brass nuts can be hard to remove!

When the mounting nuts are removed from under the sink, go topside and slowly but firmly work the faucet back and forth to break the putty seal and pull the faucet up and out of the sink holes. The sink will be a little messy when the faucet is removed, and it's important that you clean off all the old putty and debris.

After you remove the old faucet and clean the sink holes, you can mount the new kitchen faucet. Since kitchen faucets come in many styles, you'll need to follow your specific manufacturer's instructions to properly install the new faucet, especially if it's a "component" faucet that installs with individual pieces in each sink hole. Most kitchen faucets are deck-mounted, and here's how to install a deck mount:

To install a deck-mounted kitchen faucet, first start with the chrome pass-through for the spray hose. Wrap the bottom of the bell-shaped chrome ring with plumber's putty and insert it in the far-right sink hole of a four-hole kitchen sink. Under the sink, install the washer and mounting nut on the hose guide's threads and tighten with the basin cock wrench.

Once the hose guide is attached firmly to the kitchen sink, remove any excess putty and slide the spray hose with the spray head attached through the hose guide until the spray head sits in the guide.

Next, mount the faucet to the sink. To the left of the sprayer will be the three remaining open sink holes. Some faucets come with a rubber gasket, while others will call for a bead of plumber's putty for the faucet seal. Attach the gasket or putty ring to the bottom of the deck base.

Guide the kitchen faucet through the three sink holes onto the sink deck, making sure the proper components go through the correct holes. On most one-handle faucets, the built-in supply tubes and spray fitting go through the center hole and the mounting bolts go through the outside holes.

Two-handle faucets usually will have no built-in supply tubes, and

ONE-HANDLE FAUCET WITH FOUR-HOLE SINK

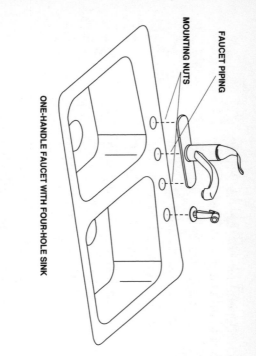

FAUCET PIPING

MOUNTING NUTS

TWO-HANDLE FAUCET WITH FOUR-HOLE SINK

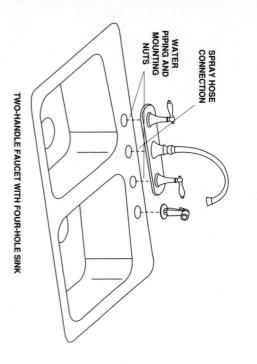

SPRAY HOSE CONNECTION

WATER PIPING AND MOUNTING NUTS

the hot connection and mounting fitting will use the left hole, the spray fitting goes in the center hole, and the cold connection and mounting fitting will use the right side hole. Push the faucet down firmly onto the sink deck.

To anchor the faucet to the sink, make sure it's sitting straight on the sink. If you tighten down a crooked faucet, you'll end up with an unprofessional-looking job! From under the sink, attach a washer and mounting nut to the threads of each mounting fitting and tighten down firmly.

If you used putty for your sink-to-faucet seal, remove any excess from around the faucet. Grab the faucet and try to move it back and forth. If it moves, you'll have to tighten it up a little more.

If the faucet is firmly in place, go back under the sink and attach the spray hose's compression fitting to the matching faucet spray fitting in the center of the faucet, using the basin cock wrench.

At this point the spray head and hose are connected to the kitchen faucet and the faucet is mounted on the sink. The last thing that needs to be connected is also the most important step of the job.

Both hot- and cold-water supply tubes need to be attached from the stop valves to the faucet connections. We'll start with the faucet connections because, depending on your style kitchen faucet, the supply tubes will hook up a little differently.

As I mentioned, one-handle kitchen faucets will usually have the three-eighths-inch supply tubes built into the faucet. Depending on the one-handle faucet, the supply tubes can be set up in three ways:

- Long, flexible, braided stainless-steel tubes with built-in three-eighths-inch valve compression fittings that attach directly to the stop valves.

- Soft three-eighths-inch open-end copper tubes that may reach the stop valves but in most cases will need three-eighths-inch compression fittings and extensions.

- Soft three-eighths-inch copper tubes with soldered compression fittings at the ends of the supply tubes for easier connections to extensions.

Two-handle faucets, on the other hand, are pretty straightforward and usually have half-inch compression connections at each hot- and cold-water inlet, allowing the use of standard flexible supply tubes.

Once you have the correct connections and supply tubes for your faucet, attach the compression fittings to your one-handle or two-handle faucet with the basin cock wrench. If your faucet has three-eighths-inch soft copper tubing for your connections, move and connect the tubing very carefully, or it can kink and ruin the entire faucet!

When the supply tubes and/or compression fittings are connected to the faucet and you've determined that the supply tubes will reach the stop-valve connections, you can now complete the job.

The last step in completing the installation of your kitchen faucet will be to connect the open ends of the supply tubes to the hot and

PRO TIP

Having a few different connections for just one type of kitchen faucet can be confusing. It's important when you purchase your kitchen faucet to open the box at the supply house and get the proper faucet connections and supply tubes that will work with your type of kitchen faucet and stop valves, or else you'll be making a return trip!

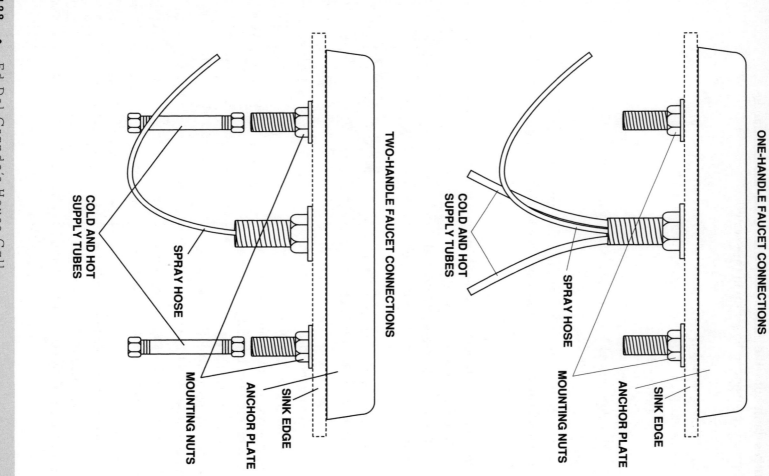

TWO-HANDLE FAUCET CONNECTIONS

COLD AND HOT
SUPPLY TUBES

SPRAY HOSE

MOUNTING NUTS

ANCHOR PLATE

SINK EDGE

ONE-HANDLE FAUCET CONNECTIONS

COLD AND HOT
SUPPLY TUBES

SPRAY HOSE

MOUNTING NUTS

ANCHOR PLATE

SINK EDGE

cold stop valves. Make sure you connect the cold-water faucet supply to the cold-water stop and the hot-water supply to the hot stop. If you cross these lines, the faucet will not work properly.

Most stop valves use three-eighths-inch compression fittings, and most flexible faucet supply tubes will have the compression fitting built into the end of the tube or have an open end that will accept a compression nut and ferrule. No matter what type of tube you use, connect the supply tubes to the stop valves by attaching and tightening the compression nuts to the valve threads.

To test the faucet and connections, make sure the faucet is completely off and slowly turn on the hot- and cold-water stop valves. Check your stop valve, supply tube, and faucet connections for any leaks. If everything looks good, move on to the faucet.

When installing a new kitchen faucet, it's normal to get a little debris in the water lines, and kitchen faucets are very sensitive to debris. I recommend flushing out the water lines, to avoid clogging up the faucet and spray head. Remove the aerator at the end of the faucet spout and slowly turn on both the hot and cold water. With the aerator removed, any debris in the water lines will flow out of the open spout and clean the lines.

After a minute or so, reattach the aerator to the spout and test the faucet to make sure that it's working properly. Also, check the spray head. If you run hot water through the spray head, it will soften up the hose a little. Work the hose in and out of the hose guide.

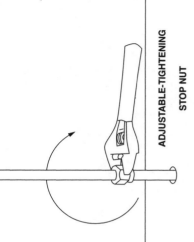

BASIN WRENCH

ADJUSTABLE-TIGHTENING STOP NUT

Final note on kitchen faucets: Most two-handle deck-mounted faucets come with standard handles that you may have to attach during installation. The reason for this is that designer handles may be purchased separately for two-handle faucets if you wish to upgrade.

SINKS AND COUNTERTOPS

These two just go together naturally! All homeowners dream about that special sink and countertop that will not only make their kitchen a practical working environment but will also enhance its beauty and style.

Let's start with the kitchen sink. Today you can get kitchen sinks that are just about any color, size, shape, and material you can think of. There are even sinks that can cook your food! Before we get into the steps of replacing a sink, it's important to know some of the choices available out there and the features of each one.

To select the type of kitchen sink that will work best for you, it's important that you keep a few things in mind:

Bowl Style of the Sink: In many homes there may be one main user of the kitchen sink. With just one person using the sink, it will be easier to organize and clear the sink for disposer use. If that's the case, a single-bowl sink may be the best choice. Single-bowl sinks offer

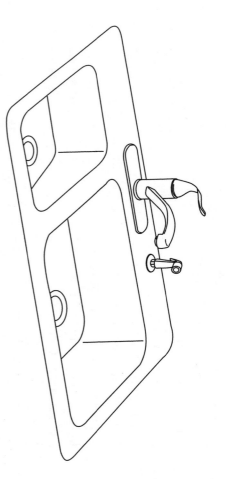

a larger bowl area and make it easier for larger pots and pans to be filled and cleaned.

If more than one person will be using the sink on a regular basis, a double-bowl sink may be the way to go. As the name says, it will "double" the workspace of the sink and/or keep one bowl clear for disposer use when multiple people are using the kitchen. However, because of the space needed for two bowls, the bowl sizes are smaller.

A happy medium for most families is the "large bowl/small bowl" setup. With this type of sink, the main bowl is as large as possible and the secondary bowl for the disposer is smaller. This offers some of the advantages of the larger single-bowl sinks and the convenience of a second bowl for disposer use.

Size of the Sink: When replacing a kitchen sink, this will be an easy choice, since in most cases the new one should be the same size as the old one, unless you plan to get a contractor involved. Measure your kitchen sink's outside edges from side to side and front to back to determine your existing sink size. For new installations measure your counter area to see what size and style will fit best in your kitchen.

Most double-bowl kitchen sinks will be the standard size, called "thirty-three by twenty-two." That means just what it sounds like. The side-to-side sink measurement is thirty-three inches, and the front to back is twenty-two inches. Smaller one-bowl sizes can be "twenty-

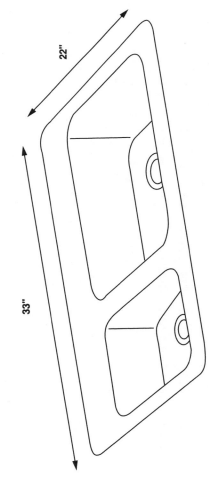

33"

22"

five by twenty-two," and larger three-bowl sizes can be "forty-three by twenty-two."

The Material Used for the Sink: There are many specialty sink materials out there, like fireclay and resin-based products. But by far the two most popular choices for kitchen sinks are cast iron and stainless steel.

Cast-iron sinks are the luxury standard in kitchen sinks, with a beautiful baked-in enamel finish that comes in many colors. If well cared for, a cast-iron sink can last the lifetime of your home. A great feature of cast iron is its strength and durability, and cast-iron sinks supply the faucet with a sturdy mounting base. The only downside to cast iron is its weight. Because it is so heavy, installation can be labor-intensive.

Stainless-steel sinks have long been thought of as the budget choice, but times are changing! Today's stainless-steel sinks feature beautiful brushed finishes, noise-reduction technology, and, most important, they're available in premium "gauge" thickness.

Gauge thickness is a number that refers to how thick the stainless steel is that's used for the sink. The lower the gauge number, the thicker the material. Low-end stainless-steel sinks can be 22 or 23 gauge, while high-end sinks can be 18 or 19 gauge.

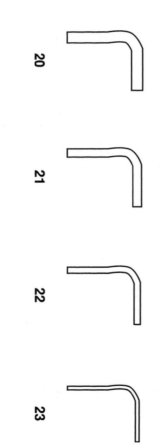

19

20

21

22

23

Replacing a Standard Kitchen Sink

Since kitchen sinks are made of many different materials and hooked up in a variety of ways, the type of replacement we'll do is for the most common and easiest to remove and install: a standard top-mounted, double-bowl stainless-steel sink using a single drain trap.

Many older stainless-steel sinks can become dented, dulled, and out of date. The good news is that it's not that difficult to change out the old stainless steel sink and upgrade to one of the new heavier-gauge models. I would also recommend changing out the old faucet as well when doing this project.

You can install the new faucet once the sink is in the counter as per the faucet instructions I gave you, or you can modify those instructions slightly to install the new faucet on the sink before you mount it into the countertop. This will allow for an easier installation of the faucet.

Tools and Materials Needed: You'll need your hand tools and large slip-joint pliers, adjustable wrenches, a very long, thin, flathead screwdriver, basin cock wrench, plumber's putty, rags, and safety glasses.

Be sure you get a new stainless-steel sink that exactly matches your existing sink's measurements. This includes bowl size, depth, and especially the location of the drain holes. Aside from the sink, you'll need your faucet with trim materials, two basket strainer kits that also match the existing drains, and Teflon paste.

To remove the old sink, start by turning off the stop valves under the sink and disconnect the faucet supply tubes completely from both stop valves (as per the faucet-changing instructions). There is no need to remove the faucet from the old sink, since the entire sink will be removed. This saves a lot of work, especially if the old faucet is rusted in place.

Self-rimming cast-iron sinks are held in place with adhesive caulking, and the caulk seal has to be broken between the counter and the sink with a hammer and a thin putty knife, which can be a tricky and time-consuming job. Stainless-steel sinks, however, are held in place with special sink clips located under the sink in grooved sink tracks.

TROUBLE NOTE

You might have to alter your drain lines to fit the new sink and, if your sink has a disposer, disconnect and reinstall the unit according to the manufacturer's instructions. Also, if you have a heavy cast-iron sink, work with a professional to be safe and avoid counter damage.

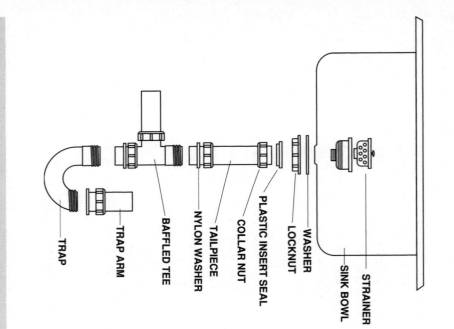

SINK TRACK

SINK MOUNTING CLIP

TRAP

TRAP ARM

BAFFLED TEE

NYLON WASHER

TAILPIECE

COLLAR NUT

PLASTIC INSERT SEAL

LOCKNUT

WASHER

SINK BOWL

STRAINER

Although these clips may be awkward to reach, they usually remove quite easily. Make sure you put on your safety glasses and, with your long, thin, flathead screwdriver, reach up under the sink and unscrew the anchor pins in the sink clips. Most pins will be slotted.

Once the anchor pins are loose, you can usually remove or turn the sink clip, and that will release it from the countertop. You need to do this with every clip under the sink to free the sink from the counter. Be careful, because the sink clips like to fall from the sink and may hit you!

With the faucet supplies disconnected and the clips removed, the only thing that should be holding the sink in place are the drain lines. Drain lines attach to the sink by means of the basket strainer assemblies. The basket strainers are mounted to the sink holes, and at the bottom of the strainer assembly are threads that the drain tailpieces attach to. Most tailpieces attach to the basket strainers with a large collar nut.

To free the sink, remove both collar nuts from the straight tail piece and the J-bend tailpiece known as a *continuous waste*. Now that both of the large nuts are off, the sink should be free.

Pull upward from the top of the sink, while grabbing the faucet for leverage. The stainless-steel sink should not have adhesive caulking holding it, so you should now be able to lift it out of the countertop. Discard the sink, faucet, supply lines, basket strainers, and old clips. Then clean up the sink hole and sink area.

Dressing the New Sink: If you hear a plumber say that it's time to "dress the sink," it doesn't mean the sink is going to a formal dinner. It means that the faucet and trim will be installed before the sink is mounted to the countertop. This makes the installation easier, because now most of the work is done in an open area instead of under the sink inside a small cabinet.

To dress a sink, start by mounting the faucet and sprayer to the sink according to your faucet manufacturer's instructions and the tips I gave you in the section on kitchen faucets. Standard kitchen sinks have four sink holes, and standard kitchen faucets use four holes.

Measure the approximate length of the flexible faucet supply lines needed to reach the stop valves from the faucet connections and install the appropriate supplies to the faucet as we also discussed earlier. The faucet should now be ready to go, with only the stop-valve compression fittings remaining to be connected once the sink is installed.

The basket strainers are next, and one will go into each drain hole. (If you're installing a disposer, one of the holes will use your disposer's mounting bracket instead of a basket strainer.) Basket strainers have five main parts:

- The strainer basket.

- The strainer body.

- The rubber pressure gasket.

TROUBLE NOTE

Be careful. If the old sink seems stuck, someone may have glued it to the countertop, and you'll need to remove the adhesive caulk seal before you can pull the sink up. Don't pull up too hard on your sink if it is stuck—you could damage the countertop.

- The fiber friction gasket.
- The locking ring or nut.

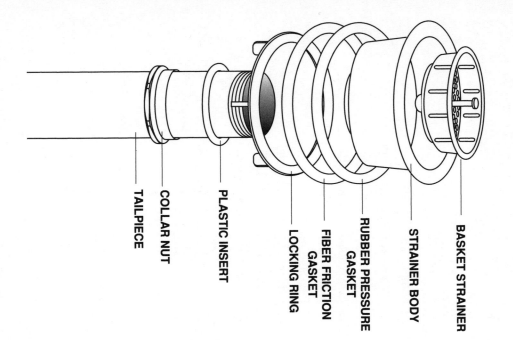

BASKET STRAINER

STRAINER BODY

RUBBER PRESSURE GASKET

FIBER FRICTION GASKET

LOCKING RING

PLASTIC INSERT

COLLAR NUT

TAILPIECE

With only five pieces, installation is a snap! Put plumber's putty on the underside of the strainer body's flange and push it into the drain hole. On the underside of the sink bowl, place the rubber pressure gasket, followed by the friction gasket. Then thread the locking nut onto the threads and tighten it up with the large slip-joint pliers. Once the strainer body is compressed to the sink hole, clean off the excess putty.

The sink has now been dressed, before placing it in the countertop. You may want to put a bead of plumber's putty around the edge of the hole to seal the sink. Plumber's putty will seal a stainless-steel sink but won't glue it to the counter, since the sink clips hold a stainless-steel sink in place. Adhesive caulking is used with self-rimming cast-iron sinks. Don't use putty on stone or porous countertops. The oils in putty can cause staining.

Place the sink in the countertop opening, being careful not to kink any supply tubes or faucet components. Once the sink is sitting flat on the counter, put on your safety glasses and go under it with the bag of sink clips and a long, flat screwdriver. It's now time to install the clips and anchor the sink.

Depending on the make and model of your stainless-steel sink, the clips may be ready to install out

of the bag or you may have to put them together. Either way, once they are ready to go, slide the clip post into the sink clip's channel and then turn the clip so the teeth of the clip bite into the underside of the countertop. Once the clip is lined up, tighten it.

Most standard stainless-steel sinks will require at least three to four clips per side. The clips pull the sink into the counter to make a tight seal, so there's no reason to overtighten the clip once the sink meets the countertop. When all the clips are installed, connect the plumbing.

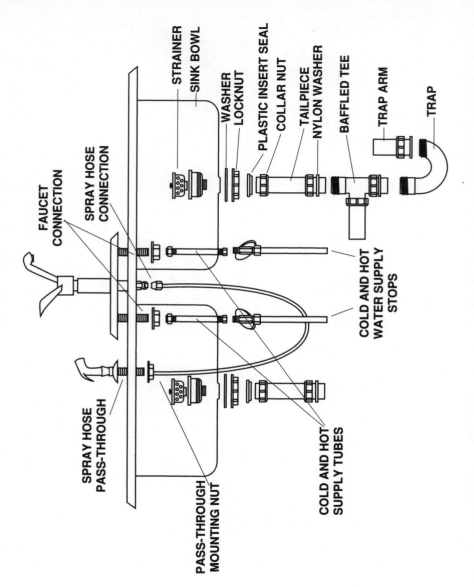

FAUCET CONNECTION

SPRAY HOSE CONNECTION

SPRAY HOSE PASS-THROUGH

PASS-THROUGH MOUNTING NUT

COLD AND HOT SUPPLY TUBES

COLD AND HOT WATER SUPPLY STOPS

STRAINER

SINK BOWL

WASHER

LOCKNUT

PLASTIC INSERT SEAL

COLLAR NUT

TAILPIECE

NYLON WASHER

BAFFLED TEE

TRAP ARM

TRAP

Start with the drain-line connections. If you ordered the new sink to the exact specifications of the old sink, you should be able to connect the existing continuous waste and tailpiece to the new basket strainers. Use the existing large collar nuts with the drain piping and insert the included tailpiece gaskets between the drain connection and strainers. Once the gaskets are in place, thread and tighten the collar nuts onto the basket strainers to complete the connection. Remember, installing garbage disposers and/or a different style sink may require some repiping of the drains.

Finish up with the water lines and connect the supply tube's compression fittings to the hot and cold stop valves. Turn on the stop valves, run the faucet, and check for leaks in the water and drain lines. After the initial test, if all looks good, you may want to give the drains a professional test by partially filling the bowls and draining them together.

Types of Countertops

Now that people are choosing different sink styles to install in their kitchens, countertop manufacturers have jumped on the bandwagon and are designing counters that will match and mount with almost any type of kitchen sink you can think of.

While under-mounting kitchen sinks has become very popular, the top-mounting sinks are still by far the standard. A top-mounted sink will allow you to change just the sink without removing the entire countertop. But in some instances, even if your sink is top-mounted, you may still want to change and upgrade your countertop. If that's the case, make sure you know my countertop basics.

There are three main choices when it comes to countertops:

CABINET FRAME

COUNTERTOP

SINK

Laminates: Most people know this as a Formica top, but that's actually a brand name. The professional term is "laminate," and it's the most popular countertop material for good reason. It's an extremely versatile material that can be installed in countless layouts, sizes, shapes, colors, and textures. Don't let the inexpensive price tag fool you. As far as I'm concerned, you get the most bang for your buck with a laminate countertop.

Natural stone: Granite is the choice for most stone kitchen countertops. It's amazing the colors you can choose from, and it's hard to believe that nature can produce so many designer color patterns. No two stone countertops are exactly the same, but you do have to pay for that originality. Stone countertops are naturally expensive.

Ceramic tile: Tile is an in-between choice for countertops, a step above laminate but not as expensive as one-piece stone counters. The drawback with tile counters is that you will see grout lines in the counter, and they can be tough to keep clean.

Engineered materials: These are high-end, stonelike solid-surface materials that are manufactured. The advantage is that since these countertops are man-made, the choice of sizes, shapes, colors, and patterns is endless! Plus, sink bowls can actually tie in to the countertop without any seams.

REFRIGERATOR DISPENSERS

Most new refrigerators have automatic ice makers that crush the ice and dispense chilled water, with taps built right into the refrigerator door. This is a real cool feature that adds value to your kitchen.

However, if you live in a home that was built years ago, before refrigerators became instant beverage dispensers, you may have no water line or feed valve installed at the refrigerator area for the necessary hookup. Or you may have a water line and feed valve in place but have no clue as to how to make the connection to the ice maker and the water dispenser.

If you fall into either one of these categories, don't worry—you can easily tie in to your home's existing plumbing system and run your own water line to the refrigerator area. Once you have a water line in place, the actual hookup can then be completed.

If you have no existing water line to the refrigerator, the first thing you need to do is locate an easy place to tap in to your cold-water piping system. "Tap in" means connecting your new water line to an existing water line. Under your kitchen sink should be the cold-water pipe and valve for the kitchen faucet. That's a good place to tap in.

Making the Tap

This is such a popular project that there are three basic ways to make the tap into the present cold-water line under your sink.

Hard Connection Hookup: This is what most pros choose, and included with the tap will be a new ice maker stop. To install this type of tap, you need to shut off and drain your entire house's water system. Cut through the copper cold-water line below the cold-water faucet stop, install a hard tee fitting for your type of pipe with a dedicated shutoff valve, and refill the system.

A hard tap with a soldered fitting and stop is considered the best connection by plumbers and is best installed by plumbers or skilled homeowners.

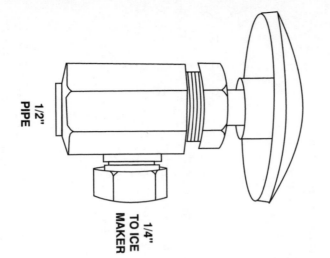

1/2"
PIPE

1/4"
TO ICE
MAKER

HARD SOLDER FITTING

Needle or Saddle Valve: This type of specialty valve is usually included with many of the ice maker kits on the market today. A nee-

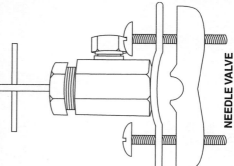

NEEDLE VALVE

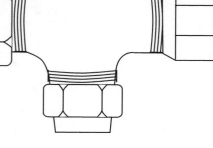

TO FAUCET

1/4"
TO ICE
MAKER

3/8"
TO STOP

dle or saddle valve will attach to a copper cold-water pipe with a special saddle clamp and gasket. Once the valve is attached to the cold-water line, you keep turning the handle of the valve clockwise until a hollow needle in the valve punches through the copper pipe to complete the tap.

Needle valves are easy to install but should be used only on ridged copper pipe. If you have a different type of pipe, use another method. Also, check your local codes. In some areas the use of needle valves may not be allowed, and you *cannot* make this type of tap.

Tap-in Tee or Maximum Tee: This specialty fitting connects directly to the threads on top of the present faucet stop and turns one outlet on the stop into two compression outlets. One outlet supplies the faucet and the other supplies the new refrigerator line. This is an easy and reliable tap for a novice or a pro to connect, and here's how to do it:

Installing the Tap-in Tee

Tools and Materials Needed: Along with a compression tap-in tee to fit your present kitchen faucet's stop, you'll need a flexible stainless-steel faucet supply, a basin cock wrench, a small adjustable wrench, a small pair of slip-joint pliers, and rags.

The great thing about this type of tap connection is that you only need to shut off the cold-water stop under your kitchen sink. Close the stop and make sure it's holding the water by opening only the cold side of the faucet.

The next step is to remove the cold-water supply line from the sink's stop valve to the faucet connection under the sink. Use the adjustable wrench to disconnect the smaller bottom connection to the stop and use the basin cock wrench to disconnect the larger compression connection of the supply line to the faucet. Have some rags handy!

Once the cold-water supply line to the faucet is removed, you will have room to install the tap-in tee.

The tee has three compression outlets: one three-eighths-inch female end, one three-eighths-inch male end, and one quarter-inch fitting to fit the refrigerator line. The female end connects to the male end on the stop. Attach the tee to the stop and tighten with the adjustable wrench. Back off the stop with the slip-joint pliers to prevent stressing the stop connection to the water line.

Also, make sure the two male ends of the tee are pointing in the right directions. The three-eighths-inch male end should be pointing up toward the faucet, and the quarter-inch male end on the side should point in the direction of the new refrigerator line.

Now it's time to install the new flexible water-supply line from the tee to the faucet. Connect the small three-eighths-inch compression end of the supply line to the tee with the adjustable wrench. Don't forget to back off the connection. Switch tools to the basin cock wrench and attach the larger end of the supply line to the standard faucet connection.

The kitchen faucet is now reconnected, but don't turn on the water! Remember, you have an open end on the new tap-in tee, and the water can't be turned on until the new refrigerator line is installed. The stop valve under the sink will now control the water for the faucet and refrigerator.

With the tap-in now completed, you have a new quarter-inch fitting to work with, and it's time to run the small quarter-inch flexible water line that will supply water to the ice maker and water dispenser.

The quarter-inch piping comes coiled up in a kit form that you can get at most home centers. The kits usually supply all the materials and trim you'll need to run the water line and make the connections. Kits include about twenty feet of flexible piping. As far as the type of piping goes, you'll have three basic choices to match your budget and skill level.

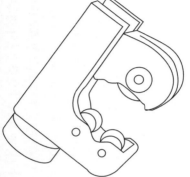

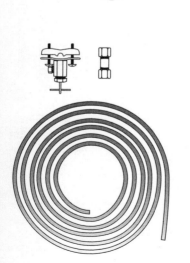

MINI TUBING CUTTER

(SOLD SEPARATELY)

COIL OF TUBING

Refrigerator Piping Choices

Plastic line: This is a very inexpensive and easy-to-work-with flexible water line. But check your local codes to see if it's approved. Plastic ice maker lines can be easily damaged, and if improper compression fittings are used, they may cut through the plastic tubing and cause a leak.

Copper tubing: This is the plumber's choice, because of its strength and durability. It's also fairly self-supporting, so in exposed areas it gives a nice, clean look. There is a price to pay for all that, both in extra costs and labor. It's a tricky pipe to work with and will kink if mishandled.

Flexible braided stainless steel: This type of pipe took the supply-line industry by storm. It combines the reliability of copper with the flexibility of plastic. Even though it's pricey, many plumbers and homeowners are discov-

PRO TIP

You may need to drill holes for this project, so get the correct-size bit for the water line you choose. Also, the best type of bit for this project is the long shaft style called a *feeler bit or pilot bit.* The perfect hole will allow the tubing to slide through easily but not give a sloppy appearance around the pipe.

ering it's a great choice. The disadvantages are that it's a little bulky and cannot be cut. The coils are not as long as the other types of tubing, so you may have to combine two kits for longer runs.

Once you pick the type of supply line that's best for you, it's time to run the line over to the refrigerator. If you're lucky and you already have a water supply and stop behind your refrigerator, you're ready for the final tie-in, but hold on. Please wait for the rest of us to catch up!

Running the Supply Line

Tools and Materials Needed: Along with your ice maker kit, you'll need a drill and proper-size bit, pipe clips, a tubing cutter, electrical tape, and help from a friend.

Obviously, every kitchen is set up a little differently. Some refrigerators may be right next to the sink, while others may be across the room from it. You may have an open basement, or you could be on a concrete slab. One way or another, you need to lay out a path through cabinets, closets, floors, walls, basements, or crawl spaces to run your water line.

Make sure you choose a fairly open area to run the water line, since you'll need to drill holes along the path for the line to follow. Don't drill in any areas where you may hit wires or other utilities!

You'll first need to drill any holes necessary for feeding the line. Put electrical tape over the tubing end to keep the line clear of debris and work backward from the refrigerator area. You'll want the water line to exit the refrigerator area as far back as possible. This way you can push your refrigerator in close and tight to the back wall.

In most homes with open basements, you can simply drill one hole in back of the refrigerator area through the floor and one hole under the kitchen sink through the cabinet and floor. Then feed the tubing down into the basement or crawl space from the refrigerator and pull it up into the kitchen sink cabinet. Help from a friend makes this job a lot easier!

If you don't have a basement or crawl space, you'll have to be a little more creative in finding a path for the water line. If your codes allow, kitchen base cabinets can provide a path for ice maker lines. Drill through the bottom rear corner of the cabinet and run the water line across the floor of the cabinet. Copper tubing works well for this application.

Keep running and snaking the tubing from the refrigerator to the sink. Once you have the line in place, secure the tubing to any joists or supports with clips for a nice, professional look and to protect the pipe. Make sure you leave plenty of tubing under the sink and behind the refrigerator so you don't come up short when you make the final connections!

Refrigerator and Water Connections

Okay, no matter if you had to run the water line loop from a tap-in tee or if you have a water line and stop valve in place behind your refrigerator, performing the final connections is the next step.

Tools and Materials Needed: Along with the compression fittings that come with the kit, you'll need a small adjustable wrench, small slip-joint pliers, and a tubing cutter.

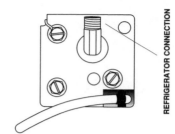

REFRIGERATOR CONNECTION

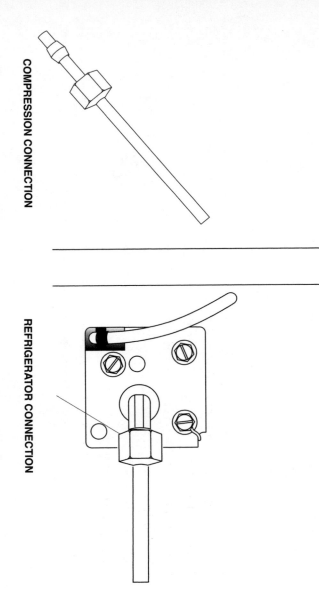

COMPRESSION CONNECTION

REFRIGERATOR CONNECTION

Again, it's always best to work backward from the refrigerator to the sink. This way, with the refrigerator hooked up first, you avoid any chance of hooking up the water at the stop valve and being turned on with an open refrigerator line. I've seen this happen!

Leave at least three coils of tubing at the refrigerator area. After the water line is connected, the extra pipe will allow you to move the refrigerator in and out from the wall. The coiled loops will act like an accordion, and the tubing will expand and contract as necessary.

First, cut away any excess piping with the tubing cutter. (Remember that braided stainless-steel piping cannot be cut.) Next, locate the refrigerator's water connection. The water connection on most refrigerators will be located at the solenoid valve, which is on the lower right side on the back of the appliance.

You can connect the refrigerator first, because purging might not be necessary if you've protected the feed end with tape, as I told you. The electrical tape on the feed side of the tubing prevents debris from entering the line. However, if you used a hard-soldered ice maker valve for your tap in, purging is a good idea to wash out any debris. Otherwise, start the connections at the refrigerator.

The ice maker kit should contain the correct compression fittings needed for the quarter-inch tubing to mount on the solenoid valve connection of the refrigerator. Follow your manufacturer's instructions for connecting your model and follow the kit instructions for connecting your type of tubing to the refrigerator.

The basic steps will be to slide the compression nut and ferrule over the quarter-inch tubing. (Braided stainless-steel tubing will have the nut and ferrule already attached.) Now slide the tubing onto the quarter-inch connection of the solenoid valve. Once the tubing has bottomed out in the valve fitting, push the nut and ferrule onto the solenoid fitting's threads and connect the fitting to the threads with your fingers.

Finally, snug up the connection with the small adjustable wrench. Be careful not to overtighten the compression fitting.

With the refrigerator connected, now move under the kitchen sink to the tap-in tee or, if you have a stop valve behind your refrigerator, you can start working there. Either way, the water-side hookups are alike. The only difference is the location of the water connection valve.

At the tap-in tee or the stop valve, cut or coil the tubing to size to fit the connection. Make sure you remove the electrical tape! If you use copper or plastic tubing, again slide the proper compression nut, ferrule, and trim onto the tubing. (As I mentioned, braided stainless is ready to go!) Attach the tubing, ferrule, and nut to the tee or stop and snug up the connection with the small adjustable wrench.

The water-line connection from the tap into the refrigerator should now be complete. However, before you slide the refrigerator into place, you need to test all the connections.

TROUBLE NOTE

If you use plastic tubing, make sure you use the plastic ferrule with the included supporting insert. A brass ferrule on a plastic line may cut into the tubing and cause a leak.

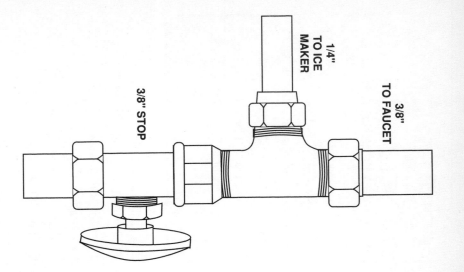

1/4" TO ICE MAKER

3/8" TO FAUCET

3/8" STOP

Slowly turn the water valve counterclockwise until it opens completely. Do a quick walk around to check for any leaks. If all looks good, plug in the refrigerator and allow the ice maker time to fill the tray. (This could take a little while.) If you have a water dispenser at the door, purge everything out by filling up a glass of water.

Once the ice maker has gone through its cycle and the water line is purged, if everything looks good, you can now move the refrigerator into place. Most big refrigerators are balanced on wheels and should slide in easily. Make sure the tubing is set up correctly to contract as you slowly push in from side to side until everything's in place.

Final Tips and Tricks with Ice Makers

Even if you have a water dispenser and you've flushed out the line, make sure you discard the first few batches of ice cubes your freezer produces. This will allow the water line to push out any remaining debris and protect you from using ice that may not be totally clean.

Speaking of clean ice, an ice maker filter is a great addition to any freezer. Filters can be installed in the new water line very easily with the same compression-fitting techniques. Whole-house water filters improve ice quality as well if installed on the main water line.

And don't forget, if you go on a long vacation, it's a good idea to turn off your refrigerator water line.

REPLACING A DISHWASHER

Replacing a dishwasher is one of those projects that looks complicated on the surface. But in reality it involves just a few basic electrical and plumbing connections!

For this project we're talking about replacing an existing dishwasher, not installing a new one from scratch. A new dishwasher installation will require extensive carpentry, electrical, and plumbing work. That job is best left to the pros.

But when replacing a dishwasher, the necessary space, water, drain, and electrical hookups that are required for the job are already in place. The replacement dishwasher can easily use the same connections.

The big question, of course, is, when should you replace your dishwasher instead of repairing it?

The answer depends on a few factors.

Age: If your dishwasher is over ten years old, unless the repair is a very simple and inexpensive one, I would not recommend investing any money in it. Usually, the way luck runs, after you make a costly repair on an older unit, something else breaks, and then you're stuck!

Value: Find out the value of your present dishwasher; it may not be a very good-quality dishwasher. If that's the case, even if the unit is under ten years old, it may not be worth the price to repair it. When dealing with an inexpensive, broken, base-level appliance that's out of warranty, your best bet is not to invest good money in a cheap unit!

New Versus Repair Costs: Finally, you may have a good-quality dishwasher that's not too old but is out of warranty. In this case you need to get a repair estimate and look up the cost of a replacement dishwasher. The rule of thumb is that if the total repair bill is more than half the cost of the new dishwasher, you may want to go with the new dishwasher.

Tools and Materials Needed: Along with your new dishwasher and hand tools, you'll need your safety equipment, assorted adjustable wrenches and screwdrivers, a noncontact electrical voltage tester, heavy-duty drop cloth, rags, Teflon tape, and electrical tape. Materials needed include wire nuts and connectors, a dishwasher drain kit, a flexible braided stainless-steel dishwasher water line, a "dishwasher 90" and trim materials like screws and clamps.

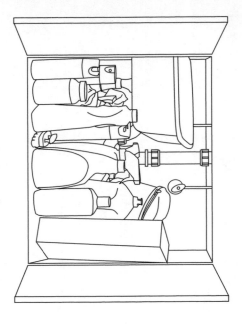

Prepping the Area: Before you even open the box of your new dishwasher, the first part of the job will be to prep the existing area so you can remove the old dishwasher and get ready for the new one.

If the space underneath your sink looks anything like mine, get ready to clean out all the junk in there that isn't nailed down. This includes things like detergents, mouse traps, dried-up sponges, and old rags. Once the sink cabinet is empty, you will be able to see the water and drain lines.

Under the sink, inspect the existing dishwasher drain line and trace the hose to the drain connection fitting. Usually a dishwasher will connect to the garbage disposer's drain fitting or the basket strainer tailpiece fitting with a dishwasher drain tee. Remove the hose clamp and the rubber hose sleeve from the drain-connection fitting.

Locate the dishwasher's water valve. Dishwashers will normally connect to a hot-water stop located next to the faucet's hot-water stop. Trace the dishwasher's water line to the correct stop valve and shut it off. You may want to shut down all the water stop valves.

Removing the Old Dishwasher: *Turn off the dishwasher circuit breaker!* With the dishwasher's electricity and water off and the hose disconnected from the sink drain you can now remove the bottom front cover panel to expose the connections.

Once the cover is off, double-check the electrical connections. Remove the electrical cover box so you can expose the wires to test and confirm that the electricity is in fact off. Use your voltage tester per the instructions to do this job. I recommend the noncontact type of tester that can sense electricity through the wire nuts so you don't have to expose bare wires.

With the power safely off, disconnect the three electrical wires from the unit. Start with the green ground wire and unscrew it from the grounding box. Disconnect the wire nuts from the black and white wires and pull them from the box as well.

You may have to remove the locking ring on the wire connector to pull the wires from the box. Once the black, white, and green wires are disconnected from the dishwasher, put the wire nuts back on the black-and-white wire tips to cover the bare ends of the wires.

Toward the front of the dishwasher, you'll find the water-line connection. It's usually a three-eighths-inch compression fitting. Disconnect the fitting nut with a small adjustable wrench and pull the water line away from the connection. Have a rag handy to wipe up any water that may spill.

Open the dishwasher door and look up under the counter. Locate the two dishwasher anchor screws that secure the dishwasher to the countertop. Remove both screws from the flanges.

Now, with a thin, flat adjustable

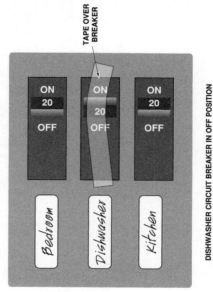

TAPE OVER BREAKER

Bedroom · Dishwasher · Kitchen

DISHWASHER CIRCUIT BREAKER IN OFF POSITION

PRO TIP

If possible, remove the doors of the kitchen cabinet as well. This will get them out of your way and give you a lot of extra working room. Reinstall the doors when you are finished.

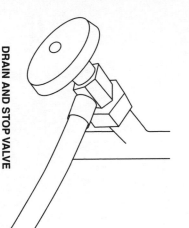

PRO TIP

When you locate the dishwasher's circuit breaker in your electrical panel, turn it off. Place a piece of tape over the breaker switch once it's off to make sure no one turns it on while you work. Also, you may have to test out a few circuits to find the exact breaker. Consult an electrician if you are unsure. Always work safely when a project involves any electrical work and never go beyond your limits.

wrench, raise the bottom lifting legs of the dishwasher. Screwing the legs up into the dishwasher will actually lower the dishwasher from the counter, giving you room to work. Once you can wiggle the dishwasher freely, it can be removed.

Protect the floor with your drop cloth and slowly pull the dishwasher out of the cabinet. As you pull, the disconnected water line and wires stay in place, while the drain hose comes out with the dishwasher.

Setting Up the New Dishwasher: Once the old dishwasher is removed and the area is cleaned and ready for the new one, you can now take the new dishwasher out of the box and set it up. Make sure you follow your manufacturer's instructions for this process.

Most dishwashers will set up with these standard steps: Take the new appliance and lay it on its back so you can get easy access to the bottom of the unit and remove the bottom cover. Locate all the water and electrical connections as per your instructions so you can get familiar with the unit.

Start with the drain hose, since most dishwashers will require you to connect the drain hose to the pump assembly. Locate the test cap on the discharge connection and remove the cap. Some water may dribble out—don't panic! Install the factory discharge hose as per instructions to the pump fitting and secure it with the clamp.

Snake the hose under and to the back of the dishwasher so you can easily push the drain hose into the kitchen sink cabinet's hole when the dishwasher is placed upright and into position. The drain hole in

DRAIN AND STOP VALVE

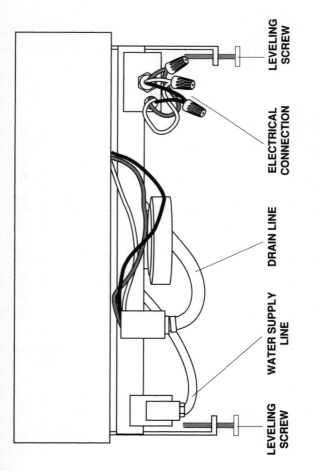

LEVELING
SCREW

WATER SUPPLY
LINE

DRAIN LINE

ELECTRICAL
CONNECTION

LEVELING
SCREW

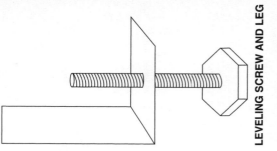

LEVELING SCREW AND LEG

the cabinet should be the upper hole in the back of the cabinet or where the old drain line went through.

Now move on to the water-inlet fitting of the dishwasher. You will need to purchase and install a fitting called a "dishwasher 90" to the threaded dishwasher female inlet fitting. Usually the dishwasher 90 will be a three-eighths-inch male thread by three-eighths-inch compression fitting.

Apply Teflon tape to the fitting threads and tighten the 90 fitting to the water-inlet threads with your adjustable wrench. Make sure the compression part of the fitting points toward the back of the dishwasher so the water line coming from under the sink can connect in a straight line to the dishwasher 90 compression side.

Open up the electrical connection box of the new dishwasher. There should be a green grounding screw or wire, a black wire, and a white wire. On the box there should also be a hole for the electrical connector and wires to enter. You may be able to use the existing wire connector attached to your wires. If not, or if there is none, now would be the time to install a new insulating wire connector to the electrical box. Insert the connector and secure it to the box with the lock ring.

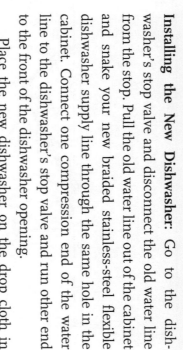

DISHWASHER THREAD

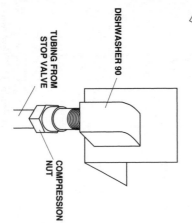

WIRING CONNECTION

DISHWASHER 90

TUBING FROM
STOP VALVE

COMPRESSION
NUT

Installing the New Dishwasher: Go to the dishwasher's stop valve and disconnect the old water line from the stop. Pull the old water line out of the cabinet and snake your new braided stainless-steel flexible dishwasher supply line through the same hole in the cabinet. Connect one compression end of the water line to the dishwasher's stop valve and run other end to the front of the dishwasher opening.

Place the new dishwasher on the drop cloth in front of the dishwasher cabinet opening. Now, slide the drain hose through the top hole in the kitchen sink cabinet. When you push the new dishwasher under the countertop, at the same time you need to pull the slack from the drain hose into the sink cabinet. Also, as the dishwasher goes into place, you have to keep the new water line and the electrical line toward the front of the dishwasher. Be careful not to kink any of the lines!

When the dishwasher rests against the back wall and is flush with the surrounding cabinets, you can lower the threaded legs to raise the dishwasher so it meets the countertop. Secure the dishwasher to the underside of the countertop with the anchor screws.

Check that electrical power is still off, then install, connect, and secure the wires to the dishwasher's electrical box as per your unit's instructions. Ground wire usually connects to the green grounding screw, black to black, and white to white, using wire nuts. Wrap both black and white wire nut connections with electrical tape, and then put the box cover on.

Connect the water line to the dishwasher 90, turn on the water, and check for leaks. Attach and clamp the rubber drain line sleeve back onto the dishwasher drain's tee fitting or the disposer connection under the sink. Loop the hose up high under the sink to prevent backflow. Check your local codes: Some areas may require backflow or vacuum breaker plumbing controls. Finally, reinstall the bottom cover panel, turn on the circuit breaker to the dishwasher, and run the dishwasher through a test cycle, and you're done!

PRO TIP

When it comes to your kitchen, the cleaner you keep your kitchen, the longer your appliances should last! Dust, grease, and grime will take a toll on your dishwasher and other kitchen appliances over the years. Ed's rule of thumb is: "If it looks new, it usually runs like it's new!

OTHER SPACES AND PLACES

DRYWALL   161

Repairing minor drywall damage   162

Repairing small holes   163

Repairing large holes   163

FLOORS   166

Installing laminate flooring   167

Laminate floor trim   169

CEILING LIGHT FIXTURES   171

Replacing a ceiling light fixture   171

WAINSCOTING   174

Installing beadboard wainscoting   175

BASEMENTS   185

Put your basement to the test   186

Controlling your "three G's" 188

Checking your gutters 188

Proper grading 189

Controlling groundwater 190

Fixing the cracks 190

Waterproofing the walls and floors 192

Sumps and pumps 193

Dehumidifiers 196

Ed's words of wisdom for other areas of our homes: "Man does not live by the kitchen and bathroom alone."

No doubt about it, the kitchen and the bathroom are the most used and talked-about rooms in almost every home. But remember the old saying about "the squeaky wheel getting the grease," and don't neglect the rest of your home just because so many repairs and improvements can be made to your kitchen or bathroom.

Any small problem or uncompleted project can turn into a big, expensive issue if left unchecked or unfinished. For example, once a customer called me to check some very bad water damage in a living room wall and ceiling. Mold had started to appear on the wall, and the ceiling's Sheetrock appeared to be rotting away.

Usually you can trace water damage on a first floor to a bathroom on the second floor. But in this case there were no bathroom or plumbing lines above the living room at all. Also, the roof didn't have any noticeable problems. So where could this water be coming from?

Almost out of options, there was only one thing left that I could do.

I opened up the ceiling and wall where the water damage was located to take a closer look. Behind the wall and ceiling, I found the two clues that I needed to solve the problem. The first clue consisted of black traces from where the water had leaked and dried over the years. The second clue was where all the traces lead back to: an electrical wire!

We all know that electrical wires can't leak water, right? So how could *this* wire be leaking water? Well, it turned out to be a very simple problem. Water was actually following the wire through capillary action.

Capillary action is a phenomenon where water can follow materials like rope or wires for long distances as long as it's going downhill.

In this case the electrical wire connected to a second-story spotlight that the owners never installed. The electrician left the wire through an unsealed hole on the outside of the house. The owners forgot about the unfinished light when they started a kitchen project.

Whenever it rained, small amounts of water followed the wire into the house through capillary action and ended up dripping on the living room ceiling located halfway across the house!

When you add up years of minor amounts of water dripping and drying with every rainstorm, you end up with major damage. The homeowners had become complacent about the hanging wire and didn't think the leak in the ceiling was a big deal—until it was too late.

Finish every project you start regardless of its location and importance before you move on to bigger and better things. My customer's kitchen came out lovely, but it was at the cost of their living room ceiling. They didn't pay enough attention to the smaller needs and potential problems of the other spaces and places in their home!

PRO TIP

DRYWALL

Whether it's a hole where a doorknob went through a wall, cracks and gouges made while moving a heavy bureau in and out of the room, or even a dent that's a reminder of a friendly wrestling match between brothers that went way out of control, drywall damage is a very common problem in most homes.

The good news is that as easily as drywall can be damaged, it can be repaired just as easily with basic skills and inexpensive materials. Repairing Sheetrock is also one of those jobs that can be relaxing and very rewarding, kind of like ironing your clothes.

You start off with an ugly-looking mess that you're ashamed to let your friends and family see, and then you realize that with a steady hand and a little time you can smooth out all your problems!

Just so there's no confusion as to what we are talking about, drywall does have several other common names. It's sometimes called wallboard, gypsum board, and the registered trademark name of Sheetrock. From here on, we will refer to it mainly as drywall, but it's all the same stuff.

Drywall is by far the most common wall surface in today's houses. There are two basic types of drywall finishes: It can be painted or textured with just the joints and screw heads filled with joint compound, or a skim coat of plaster can be applied over the entire wall surface.

Either finish can become damaged, and the repair steps are basically the same process for each one. Basic drywall damage can be summed up in three categories:

- Minor damage—includes scratches and cracks.

- Small hole—a hole in the drywall less than three inches in diameter.

- Large hole—a hole in the drywall four to twelve inches in diameter.

MINOR SCRATCH

SMALL HOLE

LARGE HOLE

Tools and Materials Needed: To repair drywall you'll need safety glasses, a dust mask, a putty knife, drywall saw, utility knife, putty knives, cordless screwdriver, straight edge, paint brush, and drop cloth. Materials will include drywall screws, joint compound, sandpaper, peel-and-stick mesh repair patches and tape, small piece of drywall, one-by-three inch wood strips, primer, and paint.

Repairing Minor Drywall Damage

For small and shallow gouges and cracks, you can simply apply a little joint compound with a putty knife to the hollow area of the drywall, let it dry, and paint. The tricky part with any drywall repair is getting the paint to match the wall. I recommend taking a paint sample from the damaged drywall area to your home center to have a small amount of new paint mixed up before you start the job.

For larger and deeper gouges and cracks, you need to do a little more work on the drywall for structure and appearance. Apply a two-inch strip of self-sticking drywall mesh tape along the gouge or crack. If the gouge or crack is curved, follow the damaged area with smaller pieces of tape and go at least and inch past the ends of the damage.

With a four-inch putty knife, push and pull

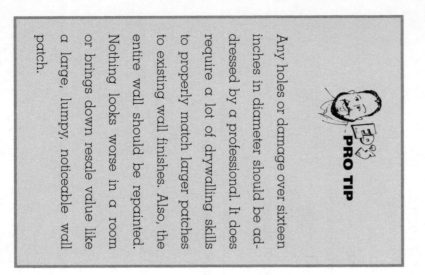

ED's PRO TIP

Any holes or damage over sixteen inches in diameter should be addressed by a professional. It does require a lot of drywalling skills to properly match larger patches to existing wall finishes. Also, the entire wall should be repainted. Nothing looks worse in a room or brings down resale value like a large, lumpy, noticeable wall patch.

the joint compound through the mesh and into the hollow areas and feather the compound into the wall until the patch is as smooth and thin as possible. It's better to go back and apply a second or third coat than to apply the first coat too thickly. Let the first coat dry for the manufacturer's recommended time.

When dry, smooth the first coat with fine sandpaper and wipe the area with a damp rag. Apply the second coat of joint compound over the first coat and repeat the process. After sanding and wiping the second coat, determine whether a third coat is necessary. If not, you can prime the repaired area and, when it's dry, apply your finish coat of wall paint.

Repairing Small Holes

A drywall hole is defined as when a section of drywall has actually been penetrated through to the back side. Structurally the drywall has also lost strength in that area. To make this repair properly, you not only have to fill in the hole, you need to strengthen the area as well. Also, make sure the hole is not any larger than three inches.

The process is almost the same as the repair of deep gouges and cracks, but for holes, you need to use a self-sticking drywall mesh patch instead of tape. Patches are usually six-inch squares, a size that will give you plenty of support and strength around a three-inch hole. Apply the patch evenly over the hole and follow the same steps as for deep gouges and cracks. Usually hole patches will require three coats of joint compound.

Repairing Large Holes

A drywall hole over four inches in diameter is a large hole. Once you have a large hole, standard fill-in repairs with mesh patches are not strong enough to support the missing section. For this you have to install new drywall backing to fill in the large hole and give the wall back its strength. Have your drop cloth ready for this job!

This type of repair will require some cutting into the existing wall, so check the area behind the wall to make sure there are no wires, pipes, or obstructions that could be damaged with a saw. The good thing about large holes is that they should allow you enough room for a visual inspection behind the wall to check for any hazards.

Take your straightedge and pencil in a square around the hole at least two inches larger than the hole itself. This is the area you need to cut. In essence you are cutting the hole out of the wall! Before you start sawing, take your utility knife and deeply score along the line. This will allow you to cut a clean edge, especially if your drywall has a plaster skim coat on it. Now with your drywall saw, slowly cut along the scored line and carefully work around any wall studs you may encounter.

When you've cut out the square and removed the pieces of broken drywall, clean and prep the edges of the opening with the utility knife so you have a nice, smooth wall opening to work with. Transfer the measurements of the opening to your new sheet of drywall and cut a section of new drywall that will fill the square in the wall.

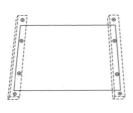

Obviously, the new drywall piece will need to be secured to the wall. If you got lucky and a wall stud is within or toward the middle of the opening, you can use the stud itself to support and hang the fill piece. If no stud is in the area, you can install two support pieces of one-by-three wood strips. Install them behind the wall with a couple of drywall screws going through the existing wall edge into the one-by-three support boards to hold them in place.

Make sure you leave at least a one-inch lip on the inside edge of the opening so you can secure the fill-in piece of drywall to the one-by-three boards. These small pieces of wood will go on opposite ends of either the top or sides of the opening. Cut and install them where they will fit best.

Now that the wall opening is prepped and framed up with the one-by-three support boards or your wall stud is exposed and in the right position, install the fill-in piece of drywall to the framing boards or stud with drywall screws to cover the opening.

Try as you might, the fill piece of drywall probably will not sit flush on every side with the existing wall, and there may be uneven gaps between the fill piece and wall. Don't worry. This is normal, and that's where your skills with joint compound will come in handy.

Once again you'll need some self-sticking two-inch mesh drywall tape. Cover each side of the repair square seams with the mesh tape. If you have a skim coat of plaster on your walls, you may even want to fill in the center of the square patch with the tape to raise the surface a bit.

When the drywall tape is in place, take your large putty knife or trowel and apply joint compound to the entire repair area and feather it into the wall. Unlike a crack or small hole, it's critical that you not only blend the joint compound with the existing wall, but you also keep the new repair area smooth and even as well.

Again the best technique is to apply a few thin coats rather than a thick, heavy, uneven coat. Sand between coats, just as for the smaller repairs. With larger repair areas, you may need at least three coats and maybe four coats of joint compound before you can prime and paint the wall.

Painting a large repair area comes with its own problems, and even if you can get the color close to the one on the existing wall, the newer paint may still stand out and look unsightly. If you paint the entire wall, it should blend into the room. However, I've seen extreme cases where the entire room had to be repainted to match the repair.

For ceiling repairs the procedure is just about the same as for a wall repair. But in most instances you need to use textured plaster instead of joint compound to blend in with the textured plaster ceilings found in many homes. Also, plan on painting the entire ceiling to cover the patch, because white is one of the toughest colors to match.

FLOORS

When it comes to installing new floors, you're frequently best off calling in a professional. Tile floors are very labor-intensive and require a lot of messy mixing work for mortar and grout. Plus, cutting tiles with a wet saw can be a challenge if you're a beginner.

Carpeting covers a floor in a hurry, but a large, heavy carpet roll and the equally heavy padding can be too much for an average homeowner to move, let alone handle and control while trying to cut the carpet and stretch it into place without leaving lumps. Also, creating a nice seam takes practice.

Solid wood floors require special and expensive nailing tools. Plus, solid wood will raise the entire height of the floor up about an inch, and that may require doing a lot of prep work, especially if it's in a kitchen and appliances have to be raised. If the wood floor is not prefinished, sanding and finishing are another tall order.

But there *is* an easy-to-install, do-it-yourself option—glueless laminate flooring. This floor installs in a snap. Literally—it actually snaps together. And a glueless laminate floor can give you a beautiful wood-like finish for much less trouble and expense than real wood.

In this country we've been using laminates on our kitchen countertops for decades. What we didn't know was that in Europe *they* were using laminates on their floors, and now we're finally catching on. Although the process for making laminate flooring is a little different from that for countertops, the floor laminates do maintain the strength, durability, and easy maintenance that we're used to with countertops. Plus, laminate floors are available in many patterns and textures.

Laminates are created with layers of resins and wood materials compressed into a plank usually around a quarter of an inch thick. It's thin but strong, so you can use laminate flooring in places where a thicker floor height may not work.

What I like best about a laminate floor is that it's a "floating floor," which means that the floor planks are locked together but not attached to the subfloor of the room, and that eliminates nailing the floor down.

Under the laminate floor there is usually a special pad that softens the feel of the floor and provides some moisture protection.

Installing Laminate Flooring

Most laminate floors install with a locking tongue-and-groove system. Following are the basics of how to lay a glueless laminate floor in your home:

Tools and Materials Needed: A jigsaw with a laminate blade, speed square, four-foot level or straightedge, small handsaw, pry bar, finish nails, nail punch, tapping block, hammer, miter box or power miter saw, measuring tape, pencil, and of course the laminate flooring and manufacturer's instructions.

There are many types of laminate floors out there, and each one has its own special tricks and installation recommendations. Laminate flooring is usually sold in packaged boxes with floor planks about four feet long and seven inches wide. Determine the square footage of your room and your home center will guide you as to how many boxes of flooring you may need. Along with the flooring, get the matching floor trim, wedges, and padding. Follow your specific instructions for installation and warranty coverage.

Removing the Old Floor and Prep Work

Before you install the laminate floor, remove any old flooring that the manufacturer does not approve to cover. You want a smooth and level surface to work with, so carpets, padding, and tacking strips will have to go. Remove floor heating and air duct covers and any floor debris as well.

Laying Down the Laminate Floor

Before installation, allow the boxes of laminate flooring to sit in the room for a day or two

PRO TIP

Roll out the laminate floor pad in small sections, then cover that area with the flooring. Roll out more padding and cover again. This will keep you from damaging any exposed padding as you walk around the room.

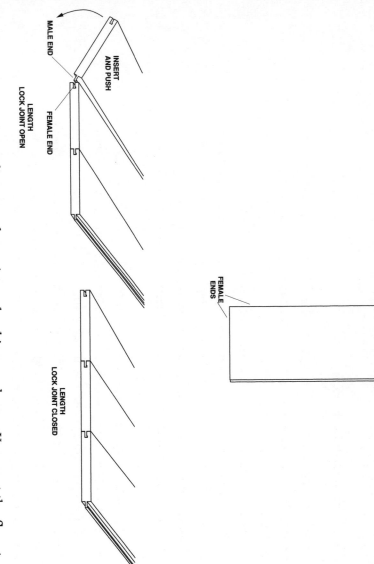

INSERT
AND PUSH

MALE END

LENGTH
LOCK JOINT OPEN

FEMALE END

LENGTH
LOCK JOINT CLOSED

FEMALE
ENDS

MALE
ENDS

to acclimate to the moisture level in your home. You want the floor to settle in to your home's environment to avoid any excessive expansion or contraction once it is installed.

Start in a corner away from the door, look at the room, and decide in which direction you want the floor seams to go. Snap the first row into place over the padding. Make sure you install the spacer wedges between the laminate floor edges and the walls to leave a quarter-inch expansion gap. Put the male end of the lock joint toward the front wall. *Note: Some floors may call for the female end to the wall.* Lock the first row together following the front wall across the room, cut the last plank to fit and complete the first row from corner to corner.

The first row is the key row and once in place, move on to the second row. The second row and all remaining rows should be installed as follows:

Start the next row with the leftover piece of the cut plank of the pre-

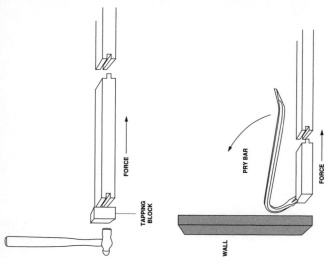

vious row. Put the cut end to the side to the wall; don't forget the expansion gap! Snap the planks *length* side edges into the lock joints of the previous row. Join the *width* side edges by putting the planks into place and hitting the tap block against the planks to force the *width* side joints together. When you get to the last piece in the row, cut the plank to fit, lock in the *length* side, and use the pry bar against the wall to squeeze the *width* side seam together.

Keep locking the planks together row after row and carefully cut around any air duct holes, radiators, or door openings. Measure often from side to side to make sure the floor is going in as straight as possible. Also, stagger the *width* side floor seams so that they are at least a foot from each other.

Once you get to the last row in the room, chances are that the plank width will be too wide to fit the very last piece into place. This time you'll have to mark the plank lengthwise with the four-foot level or straightedge and cut lengthwise with the jigsaw. Make sure you measure from the side with the locking tongue, so the plank will lock into place with the rough edge at the wall.

When the entire floor is laid down and locked together, go around the perimeter and remove the spacer wedges. It's now a "floating" floor and ready for the trim work.

Laminate Floor Trim

Laminate floors have become so popular that these days just about every manufacturer will have trim kits and or accessories available to match any style of floor. Trim accessories include:

- *Baseboard molding*—If you removed your old baseboard in the room or if you started from scratch with a new room, you can install matching baseboard to complement the floor.

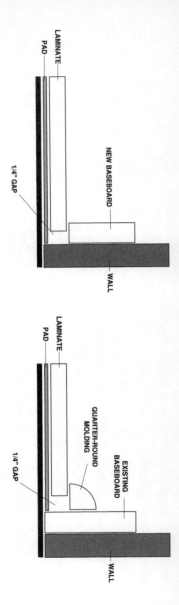

LAMINATE
PAD
1/4" GAP
NEW BASEBOARD
WALL

LAMINATE
PAD
1/4" GAP
QUARTER-ROUND MOLDING
EXISTING BASEBOARD
WALL

- *Quarter-round molding*—If you leave your present base-board in place, the quarter-round molding laid at the bottom of the baseboard will cover the expansion gap between the floor and the baseboard. The laminated quarter-round will match the floor exactly and blend right in.

- *Thresholds*—Made with the same materials as the laminate floor, the thresholds will match the new floor and provide a transition between it and existing floors in the house. The special thresholds come in various configurations to match different floor heights. Also, if you butt the floor to an existing threshold, tee-joint couplers are available to seam the laminate floor to the threshold.

- *Custom caulk*—Along with all the trim materials, manufacturers offer custom-color caulking to match the floor to fill in and hide cut marks and gaps.

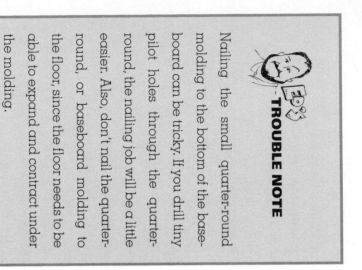

TROUBLE NOTE

Nailing the small quarter-round molding to the bottom of the base-board can be tricky. If you drill tiny pilot holes through the quarter-round, the nailing job will be a little easier. Also, don't nail the quarter-round, or baseboard molding to the floor, since the floor needs to be able to expand and contract under the molding.

In most cases you can use a combination of forty-five-degree miter joints for corners and butt joints for straight runs when installing the quarter-round and/or baseboard around the perimeter of the floor. Also, countersink all the finish nails. The laminate trim cuts pretty easily with a fine-tooth handsaw. You can use a simple miter box with your handsaw for all your joint cuts if a power miter saw is not available.

CEILING LIGHT FIXTURES

All rooms—whether it's the dining room, living room, or another space— use some type of ceiling light fixtures. In many cases the light fixture will be the center of attention.

If you're moving into an existing house, building a new home, or just giving an old room a fresh new look, chances are you'll want to replace some lighting fixtures to reflect your personality. Once you pick the perfect accent fixture, use the steps below along with the fixture instructions to install it.

Replacing a Ceiling Light Fixture

Tools and Materials Needed: Along with your light fixture and the manufacturer's instructions, you'll need coated pliers, wire strippers, screwdrivers, fiberglass stepladder, electrical tester, safety glasses, wire nuts, and electrical tape.

Removing the Existing Ceiling Fixture: The first and most important step is to make sure all electrical power is off to the light fixture. Since light fixtures usually have switches to turn them on and off, it is tempting to just shut off the switch and start the job. Don't give in to temp-

PRO TIP

Never install a light fixture that is heavier than your existing ceiling fixture. All light fixtures attach to a ceiling electrical box, and the box needs proper support to hold the weight of the fixture. Sometimes it can be hard to tell how strong a fixture box is anchored into the ceiling. A fixture that weighs the same or that is lighter than the old one should be within the limits of that box. Remember, when in doubt about any aspect of removing, hanging, or wiring a light fixture, always consult a licensed electrician and follow your local building codes.

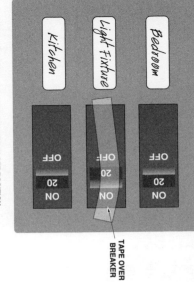

LIGHT FIXTURE CIRCUIT BREAKER IN OFF POSITION

TAPE OVER BREAKER

tation! The proper way to shut off the power to the fixture is at the panel box circuit breaker.

Turn on the light and make sure the light comes on to verify power. Shut down the correct breaker in the panel box, verifying that the fixture light has gone out due to the breaker's being shut off. Place tape on the closed breaker to keep it in the "off" position. Now shut off any wall switches that control the fix-

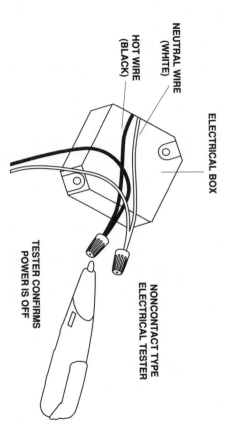

NEUTRAL WIRE (WHITE)

HOT WIRE (BLACK)

ELECTRICAL BOX

TESTER CONFIRMS POWER IS OFF

NONCONTACT TYPE ELECTRICAL TESTER

ture and tape them in the "off" position as well.

Line up the stepladder and remove any glass globes or covers from the fixture base to expose the lightbulbs. Remove the bulbs and look for the mounting screws or nuts holding the base to the ceiling electrical box. After the fasteners are removed, slowly work the base and wires out of the box and downward from the ceiling.

Once the old fixture is opened up and the wiring and wire nuts are exposed, use your electrical tester per its instructions to double-check that power to the fixture is indeed off before touching or disconnecting any wires. I recommend using the noncontact type of electrical tester that will read power through the wire nuts. This way no bare wires are exposed for testing.

With the power off and the wires safe to work with, remove the wire nuts and disconnect the black, white, and ground wire from the fixture. If the ground is connected to the electrical box in the ceiling, you may be able to leave the ground wire in place. Grounded ceiling boxes can usually ground the fixture through the metal mounting stud connections for the new fixture. Double-check to confirm that with the new fixture's instructions.

With the wires now disconnected and the old fixture removed, reinstall the wire nuts on the bare ends of the black and white wires in the ceiling's electrical mounting box.

Installing the New Ceiling Light Fixture: Follow your manufacturer's instructions for attaching the fixture-mounting kit to the ceiling electrical box. Some mounting systems use a metal strap going diagonally across the ceiling box, with mounting bolts on each side. Others may have a hollow nipple in the middle of the strap to run wires and hang the fixture. There may also be a grounding connection as well.

With the mounting kit prepped and installed, you can now wire the

PRO TIP

Check the existing wiring for proper installation. White wire should connected to white wire, black wire to black wire and green or bare wire to the ground plate. If wiring is not installed properly or looks confusing because of multiple wires, stop at this point and consult an electrician. An improperly wired fixture can lead to a potentially dangerous situation when correct installation is attempted!

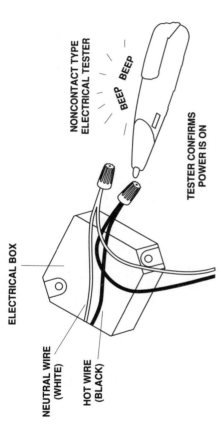

ELECTRICAL BOX

NEUTRAL WIRE (WHITE)

HOT WIRE (BLACK)

NONCONTACT TYPE ELECTRICAL TESTER

BEEP BEEP

TESTER CONFIRMS POWER IS ON

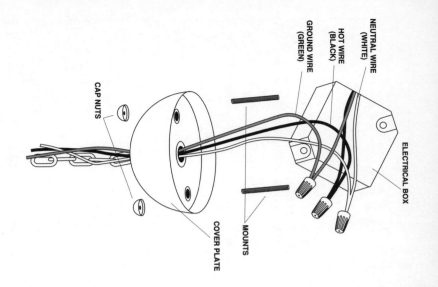

NEUTRAL WIRE
(WHITE)

HOT WIRE
(BLACK)

GROUND WIRE
(GREEN)

ELECTRICAL BOX

CAP NUTS

COVER PLATE

MOUNTS

fixture base. Most fixture bases should be prewired with a black and a white wire stripped and ready to go. Test for no power once again and attach the wires from the ceiling box to the new fixture base per your instructions. Remember, black to black, white to white, and green to ground. When the wire nuts are secured, wrap the connections with electrical tape.

Now, here's the tricky part. The mounting kit is in place and the fixture is wired and ready to be installed. However, there may be about six inches of wiring that needs to be coiled up and tucked into the box. When you push the base up to the ceiling, the mounting studs will poke through the fixture base holes. If the unit does not sit flush against the ceiling, start over, rearrange the wires, and try again!

Secure the base to the mounting box with the cap nuts. Hanging fixtures will require extra work at this point. Flush-mount fixtures can simply be finished up with the installation of the lightbulb and glass canopy. When the fixture trim work is completed, turn the power back on at the breaker and try out your new light. If the breaker trips, consult an electrician.

WAINSCOTING

Painted Sheetrock walls lack the opulent feeling that one used to get when entering a fancy living room or dining room. Gone are the days of heavy curtains, grand sofas, and plush carpets.

While I admit that keeping a room like a museum is no longer practical, that doesn't mean you can't add a nice, decorative addition to

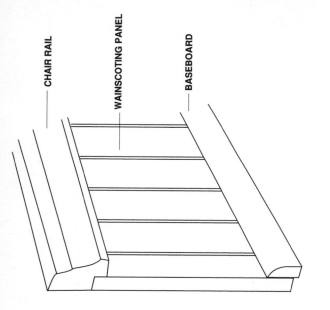

CHAIR RAIL

WAINSCOTING PANEL

BASEBOARD

spruce things up a bit! Wainscoting is a very easy project that can really transform any room. The great thing about wainscoting is that you can apply it directly over existing walls. Plus, it adds strength and durability to the wall.

Wainscoting is a wall treatment that is similar to paneling but installed on the lower part of the wall only. It comes up from the floor about thirty-three or thirty-four inches. The top edge of the wainscoting is usually trimmed with a chair-rail molding that makes the transition into the existing wall.

Professional woodworkers often build their wainscoting from scratch with deep, rich, solid wood components. Although it's beautiful, custom wainscoting is very expensive and not practical for most homeowners to afford and install.

The alternative is thin-sheet panels like beadboard or even prefabricated panels with some trim work and decorative touches built in. The beadboard paneling is the most popular and easiest-to-work-with material for wainscoting. Here's how to install it:

Installing Beadboard Wainscoting

The first thing you need to know is what beadboard is and why it's such a good choice for wainscoting. Beadboard is basically an unfinished quarter-inch (or less) wood panel that's finished on one side with faux tongue-and-groove wooden slats and seams.

The grooved lines run vertically and alternate one-and-a-half-inch-wide sections with eighth-inch spacers between the faux slats. Panels come in four-by-eight-foot sections, but many home centers offer smaller half sections that will be even easier to work with.

Because of the vertical-lined pattern, it's very easy to join two sheets together without creating a noticeable seam. Also, the lines make a great guide for cutting straight lines from top to bottom. Beadboard can be stained, painted, or left natural with a clear finish, to match any room.

Tools and Materials Needed: Along with the beadboard sheets, you'll need top chair-rail molding, bottom baseboard molding (optional if existing can be used), inside and outside corner moldings, panel adhesive, one-and-a-half-inch to two-inch finish nails, sandpaper and caulking. Along with your hand tool kit, you'll need a stud finder, nail set, two-foot and four-foot levels, tape measure, flat bar, miter saw, drill and wood bits, jigsaw, and safety glasses.

Preparing the Living Room: Clear the room by removing as much of the furniture as possible and take all loose items off the walls. Also, cover the carpets or flooring with drop cloths. Trust me: The last thing you want to do is drop construction adhesive on your rug!

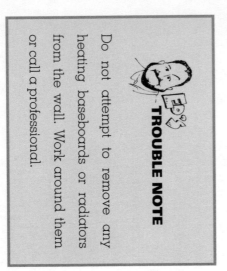

TROUBLE NOTE

Do not attempt to remove any heating baseboards or radiators from the wall. Work around them or call a professional.

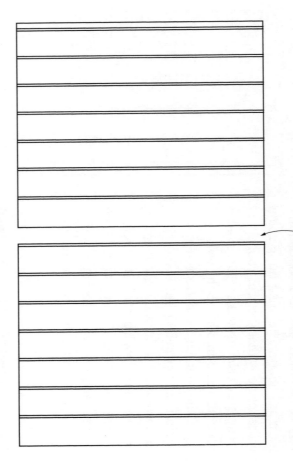

SEAM HERE

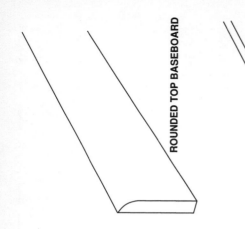

ROUNDED TOP BASEBOARD

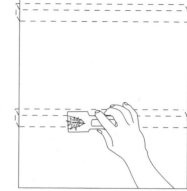

FLAT TOP BASEBOARD

Check the wooden baseboards to see if they can remain in place. Antique-style and expensive custom baseboards are best left in place, as well as any baseboards that have a flat top. You may want to demo and remove simple round-top baseboards that will not match up with the flat wainscoting panel base. Use the flat bar and a hammer for this.

Locating the Wall Studs: To install wainscoting correctly, you do need to anchor the panels to the wall studs in addition to applying adhesive to the panels. This means that you need to locate and mark the studs where the wainscoting will be applied.

A good-quality stud finder will make this job very easy. Remember that the wainscoting will rise from the floor to a height of around thirty-three inches. This means that you need to mark the vertical stud lines anywhere from thirty to thirty-six inches, so the pencil lines will be visible once the panels are in place. After the job is complete, you can remove or paint over the marks.

Start in a left-hand corner of the room and use the stud finder as per your specific tool's directions. When a stud is located, mark it appropriately on the wall. Wall studs should be installed sixteen inches on center, which means that every sixteen inches you should find a stud. Keep going to the right until you locate and mark all the wall studs that will be covered.

Prepping the Walls: You will need to create a smooth surface on the wall to accept the paneling. Any outlet covers, telephone jacks, screws, or nails need to be removed, so that nothing is sticking out farther

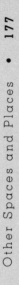

than the wall. Remember, you're removing outlet covers only—do not touch the electrical outlets themselves and be careful around open outlet boxes.

Once the wall is clear of all protruding objects, it's also a good idea to wash the wall with a mild grease-cutting cleaner to remove any oils or debris. Panel adhesive will be used on the walls, and soiled walls may not give the adhesive a strong surface for bonding.

With the studs marked and the walls prepped, you can now decide on the height of your wainscoting. Acceptable heights are anywhere between thirty to thirty-six inches, not including chair-rail height.

Marking the Perimeter: Once you choose the proper height for your wainscoting, you need to mark the top height by penciling a horizontal line around the perimeter of the room.

PRO TIP

Finding wall studs can be a lot harder than it sounds. To confirm that you've found a stud, you can gently tap a nail through the drywall to feel for the wooden stud. Make sure that you test-nail in an area that will be covered by the wainscoting. Also, watch out for pipes or wires that may be located behind the walls and avoid those areas.

This line will be your guide for measuring the height of the panels that need to be cut. If you laid out your stud lines properly, the perimeter line will intersect the stud lines at ninety-degree angles, and that will blueprint the entire job.

You can pencil this line with a level or, if you have two people working, snap a chalk line. Start in the middle of each wall and mark the desired height of the wainscoting from the floor. Even if you're leaving your present baseboard in place, make sure you measure off the floor.

With one edge of the four-foot level held at that height, draw a level line to the left and right of the mark. Move the level to the ends of the new line and proceed down the length of the wall in both directions until you create one continuous level line across the wall. Do this to every wall in the room until you have a complete perimeter line around the room.

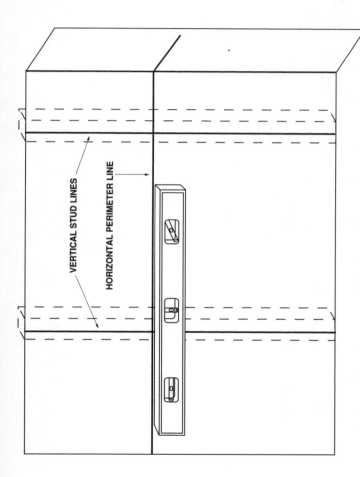

VERTICAL STUD LINES

HORIZONTAL PERIMETER LINE

Installing the Beadboard Panels: Start on an outside corner and work your way into the left- and right-hand inside corners; then go from there in both directions. If you don't have any outside corners, start on an inside corner and work your way down the wall till you hit the next corner in the room. Look at each wall as a separate project. If you install every wall correctly from corner to corner, the entire room will match up.

The goal is to have the seams between each beadboard panel fall on the centerline of a stud to create a flat joint when both sides are nailed into the stud. Four-foot panels should cover stud to stud. Correct corner-to-stud layout, measuring and cutting of the first and last panels on a wall, should achieve this goal. Always have the rough side of the cut to the corner. This way the factory-cut edges will create a tight seam.

If you removed the wooden baseboards, you will need to measure from the floor to the perimeter line on each side of the panel length for proper height. If you're leaving the existing baseboard in place, measure

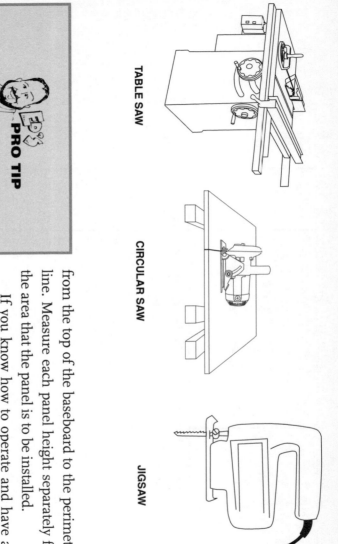

TABLE SAW

CIRCULAR SAW

JIGSAW

from the top of the baseboard to the perimeter line. Measure each panel height separately for the area that the panel is to be installed.

If you know how to operate and have access to a table saw or circular saw, use one of those tools for a professional straight cut. But if you have limited experience with power tools or if you're on a tight budget, a jigsaw can do the job. As power tools go, jigsaws are very easy to handle and are usually fairly inexpensive to purchase.

The downside is that unless you have the skills of a surgeon, you won't get a perfectly straight cut with a jigsaw. For now, though, don't worry about that, because later I'll show you tricks that will let you hide wavy cuts under moldings, baseboards, caulk, and paint.

If possible, I do recommend getting the smaller, half-size bead-board panels to minimize cutting. In some cases a half-size beadboard panel may not have to be cut horizontally at all! Whatever size panel you have, you need to transfer the floor-to-perimeter line, or measurements from the top of the baseboard to the perimeter-line measurements, to the panel itself.

PRO TIP

Jigsaw blades are available in just about every size, shape, and specialized types for different materials to be cut. Check with your home center and make sure you get a jigsaw blade recommended for thin wood paneling.

Transfer the vertical height measurements from the wall to the left and right sides of the beadboard. Have the finished side of the panel facing you. Using the four-foot level, connect the measured marks and draw a straight line horizontally across the four-foot panel. Work slowly and safely wearing your safety glasses, and cut along the line with your jigsaw.

Now that your panel is cut to height, bring it to the wall for a test fit. If you removed your baseboard, place the rough cut on the floor and the factory cut along the wall perimeter line. If you kept your baseboard, place the factory cut on the top of the baseboard and put the rough cut to the perimeter line. This will hide the rough cuts later on.

With the height all set, make sure your first piece goes from the corner to the center of a wall stud. Use your perimeter lines and stud marks to determine this. Some walls may not require panel cutting till the last piece is in place, while others may require cutting from the start.

If the first panel needs to be cut, turn the panel backward so the finished side now faces the wall. Using the four-foot level, mark a vertical line down the rough side of the panel at the wall stud and cut the panel to width. Flipping the panel to measure and cut will keep the horizontal rough cut in place and the vertical rough cut in the corner. This allows the straight factory cuts to fall on the studs when the panel is hung finish side out. This pro trick will create nice seams.

Test-fit the completely cut panel with the rough-cut side to the corner and the straight factory cut level on the center of

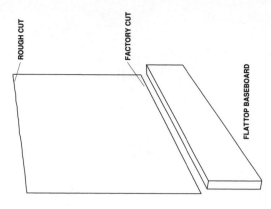

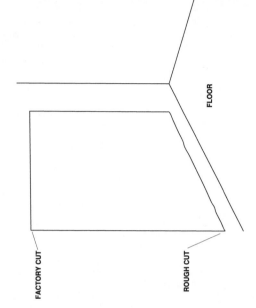

FACTORY CUT TO SEAM

ROUGH CUT TO CORNER

FLOOR

the wall stud. If all looks good, apply panel adhesive and secure the first panel to the wall by nailing and setting the finish nails at key stud points.

To cut around any outlets, phone jacks, or windows, you can transfer the measurements to the wainscoting panel and hope for the best, but I recommend getting some large pieces of cardboard or posterboard and making a template sheet with all the cutouts and then tracing the openings from the template to the panel.

Once the square cutouts are marked, use the power drill with half-inch wood bits to drill out all the corners. Then, with the jigsaw, cut from corner hole to corner hole to make the cutouts. The cutouts should be tight, because the outlet covers need to cover the panel edges.

Outlets and phone jack cover plates should have enough flexibility with the mounting screws to allow the covers to be moved out about a quarter of an inch to match the thickness of panel boards. If not, you may have to get cover plate extension screws. Make sure the outlet circuits are off when you're working around them!

Once the first corner piece is installed, you should not need to cut for width again until you hit another corner. Keep the panels level, with all seams as tight as possible, and repeat the hanging process until the wainscoting is installed along the entire perimeter line of the room. Don't sweat the small gaps—caulk, paint, and moldings should cover them up!

With the wainscoting panels in place the "rough carpentry" part of the job is complete. To hide the wavy cuts and gaps you'll use moldings and baseboards; this is called "finish carpentry."

Installing the Baseboard: If you removed the old baseboard, this means that any rough beadboard panel cuts are toward the

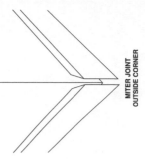

BUTT JOINT
INSIDE CORNER

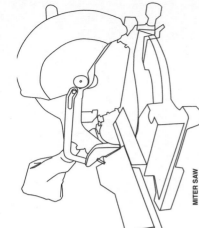

MITER JOINT
OUTSIDE CORNER

MITER SAW

floor. Installing new baseboard around the room will cover up the rough saw cuts and finish the area where the floor meets the wall.

The trick to installing baseboard is to get half-inch, squared, plank-milled baseboard so that all the corners and seams match up nicely. Complicated three-piece baseboards with scrolls and rounded designs may look nice, but they are tough to match up and can be expensive!

By using square-plank baseboard, you can install simple butt joints. Butt joints are two squared pieces of wood butted against each other to create a flat seam. Butt joints work great on inside corners and wall joints and will eliminate the need to cut forty-five-degree angles. You can butt-joint any inside-to-inside pieces of baseboard. For outside corners you should "forty-five" the ends to hide rough wood edges.

To install baseboard you'll need a miter saw. It's best to rent or purchase a power miter saw for the finish carpentry work, since hand miter saws can be very labor-intensive. If you choose to go with the power miter saw, use all safety gear and follow proper operating instructions.

Start by installing the square baseboard on any outside corners. Get a piece of baseboard that will butt tightly from the inside corner to at least four inches past the outside corner. Mark the baseboard exactly even with the outside corner. This mark will be the starting point of the forty-five-degree cut angling out and away from the corner mark.

Measure and cut the opposite side of the outside corner the same way. When dry-fitted, the two forty-five-degree pieces should wrap

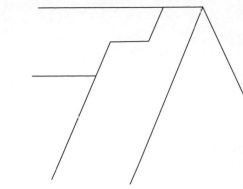

Installing the Moldings: Think of the chair rail simply as a higher baseboard molding on top of the wainscoting. However, chair rails can be a little more decorative and you may want to "forty-five" cut the inside corners as well as the outside corners. Just keep the shape of the molding simple and follow the same basic installation tips as for the baseboard.

The pro trick to installing chair rails on wainscoting is to make sure the molding you purchase has a "rabbet" cut on the bottom side of the chair rail. A rabbet cut is a square notch that runs down the entire length of the molding. The top edge of the beadboard should fit into that groove. Basically, it's putting a finish cap on the top of the wainscoting.

This little rabbet trick will do two things that'll make your wainscoting look as though a professional installed it. First, if you kept your old baseboard paneling in place and have the rough edge of the beadboard paneling on top, the rabbet groove should cover the wavy saw cuts. The deeper the groove, the more it will cover. Second, if your paneling is not completely level, the rabbet cut will give you a little leeway to raise and lower the chair rail over the panel edge to create a level line with the molding around the room.

around the outside corner with the ninety-degree sides butting directly into each inside corner. For very long runs, you may have to splice two pieces of molding together. You can butt-splice, but for a pro look try to splice with male and female forty-five-degree angles to create what's called a *scarf joint.*

Once the baseboard is dry-fitted around the room, finish-nail it to the studs and move on to the upper chair-rail molding.

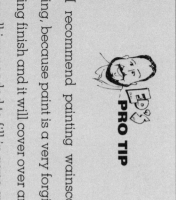

PRO TIP

I recommend painting wainscoting, because paint is a very forgiving finish and it will cover over any caulking needed to fill in gaps and spaces. Stain and poly can highlight flaws and cutting mistakes. Also, most stains don't cover over caulking well. So take some of the pressure off your project and paint your panels!

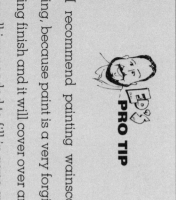

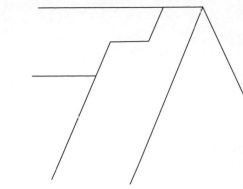

After you test-fit a section of chair rail, level and finish-nail the molding into the studs as you go around the room. When the chair rail is completed, you can install the inside corner moldings to hide the inside corner seams and outside corner moldings to wrap around any outside corner seams. Corner moldings are very delicate, and you may want to use dabs of construction adhesive instead of nails to attach these.

Once the panels, baseboard, and moldings are in place, it's time to complete the job! There is an old saying in carpentry: "Cut to fit, caulk to fill, paint to cover." I love that adage, because it says everything you need to know about finishing wainscoting, especially the last part—"paint to cover"!

BASEMENTS

Every house needs a foundation to be built on top of, so all homes have a basement, crawl space, or slab underneath them.

The reasons for choosing one type of foundation over another will depend on your location, soil conditions, and/or budget for building the home. An eight-foot-high full basement with a concrete floor under your house is considered to be the best investment option of the three. But that's not always possible.

If you've got a crawl space or a slab foundation, you have the advantage of never having to worry about fixing up your basement! If you do have a basement that can be turned into living space, it can be a good investment—providing you prep the basement properly.

A full basement can give a homeowner a place to expand. On the average you can gain about 30 percent more living and storage space

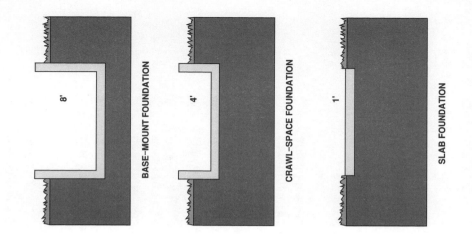

8'

BASE-MOUNT FOUNDATION

4'

CRAWL-SPACE FOUNDATION

1'

SLAB FOUNDATION

by remodeling a basement. But basements can be very wet areas, and remodeling a wet area without careful preparation can lead to problems. Before you put up one wall or cover up any concrete, check your local codes. When fixing up a basement, you need to prep and water-proof your foundation so it stays nice and dry.

Even if you don't do any actual remodeling, drying out and prepping your basement can head off foundation and water damage to your home. Also, having a treated, dry basement gives your home 10 to 15 percent more value than if your home has a wet basement.

The good news about prepping a basement is that it really isn't a hard project. It's just a series of tips, tricks, and small jobs all put together to create one very good result for your home: a dryer basement. This project is one that you can complete over a few weekends one step at a time, and it's actually a pretty relaxing job! Here's how to do it:

Put Your Basement to the Test

This old trick is the first step in drying out your basement. It's a test to determine where the source of the dampness is coming from. Dampness can be generated from inside the house or from outside.

Get a two-foot-square piece of plastic sheeting and tape it to the inside of one of your below-grade concrete basement walls with heavy-duty waterproof tape. Make sure all edges are completely sealed up. Wait a day or two before inspecting the plastic sheet. If you feel water droplets on the outside of the plastic—the side away from the wall—the moisture source can be inside your home, and you need to check and address the following:

- *Find a way to draw inside airflow to your basement from up-stairs.* Basically it's as simple as keeping the door open from the upstairs to the basement, but in most cases that's not a practical solution. So you can install a door vent to allow air to pass through the door when it's closed, or replace a solid door with a venting door.

- *Make sure your dryer vents outside, not inside your basement.* Having a clothes dryer that vents the moist air directly to the basement is like dumping a bucket of water in your basement every time you dry clothes. Venting the dryer to the outside will really cut down the moisture level in your basement.

- *Don't hang wet clothes or store stuff like green wood in your basement.* Green wood is new wood from the lumberyard that is very wet and has not yet dried out. Things like wet clothes or wet wood, even firewood, will give off a lot of moisture as they dry out.

- *Check that fueled heating equipment has proper outside airflow.* Fuel-burning equipment needs fresh air from an intake vent or drafts from openings and small gaps in your basement. Have a technician check your fuel-burning equipment to make sure you have enough fresh air entering your basement so that your equipment will run safely and to cut down moisture levels in the basement from stale air.

- *If you have a sump drain-hole basin in the floor, install a sump cover.* Sumps are nothing more than "wet" holes in the basement floor and should always have a cover over them for safety and moisture containment. A sump cover helps to trap the moisture in the sump pit, cutting down evaporation of the water into the basement.

If you peel back the plastic and feel water droplets between the wall and the plastic, you have a dampness problem due to water that's penetrating your foundation from outside the home. Water entering from outside the foundation is usually caused by the "Three G's."

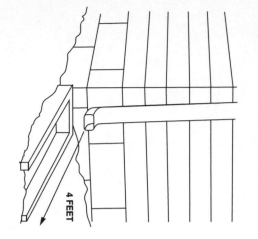

4 FEET

If you have your downspouts just spilling onto the ground in front of your foundation, you've defeated the whole purpose of your gutter system. The large amounts of water coming down the spout can now saturate the soil around the foundation, and all that water can easily work its way back into your basement.

You might be saying, "Hey, Ed, what the heck are the Three G's"? Well, I want you all to talk like professionals, and you can start by using some of the fun contractor lingo. The term "Three G's" is an old contractor's phrase that refers to the three most likely causes for water getting into a basement, and they all start with the letter G.

The "Three G's" refer to a home's gutter, grading, and groundwater conditions. The easiest way to keep a basement dry is by diverting water away from the foundation. Addressing and controlling the Three G's will increase the value of your home by creating a dryer, more comfortable living environment in your basement.

Controlling "Three G's"

Checking Your Gutters

Gutters should surround the perimeter of your house and are designed to collect the rainwater from the roof and pipe it away from your house's foundation. For a gutter system to work properly, the downspouts need to carry the water at least four feet away from the foundation. Did you know that?

Here's how to fix your gutter drains: First, you can simply install downspout extensions and/or splash pads at the ends of the downspouts. They really do work! The second way is better, but a big job. Dig out trenches around the downspouts to install underground PVC gutter drains that run out

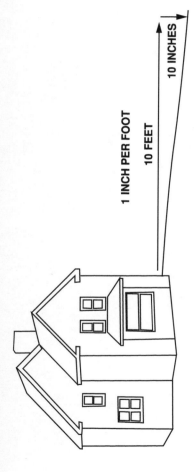

1 INCH PER FOOT

10 FEET

10 INCHES

to a main collection area away from your foundation. Either way, downspouts that are piped off correctly should solve gutter problems.

Proper Grading

Grading refers to the slope of the land going away from a house, and it needs to go in a downward direction. Any soil that slopes toward a foundation can now divert rainwater into the basement, a condition that's referred to as a "negative grade." On average the grading of the soil around a house should slope downward at one inch per foot for at least five feet away from the foundation.

The nightmare grading issue can be a concrete patio that's pitched toward a house's foundation with a negative grade. Since concrete will not absorb rainwater the way soil will, all the water can now be diverted by the patio with funnel-like action into the basement. In cases like this, the patio has to be jacked up or removed and proper grading installed.

Most grading issues can be fixed with the simple addition of more soil to low areas around your home, then blending the filled areas into the natural slope of your yard. The ideal slope should carry as much water as possible away from your home and off your property. Be careful, though. You don't want to upset your neighbors by having your entire yard drain into their property!

Controlling Groundwater

Groundwater is the most difficult of the G's to address, since you cannot stop true groundwater. Groundwater is a force of nature—like an underground river. The best you can do with a river is to divert it and control it rather than trying to figure out how to get rid it, because it won't stop! If you are unfortunate enough to live in the way of one of these underground streams, don't worry. There are ways to tame the river wild!

Fixing the Cracks: Think of your basement as a watertight in-ground swimming pool. But you don't want *this* pool to hold water—you want *this* pool to keep the surrounding groundwater out. So, just as when you're trying to repair a pool, the first step is to seal up any large cracks or holes in your basement walls. Patching holes or cracks on a vertical concrete wall is a unique process requiring special materials. Here's how to do it:

Tools and Materials Needed: You'll need a stiff wire brush, bucket, trowel, safety glasses, mask, gloves, small sledgehammer, and chisel. For materials the secret ingredient will be hydraulic cement. Hydraulic cement will stay in place when applied to a foundation wall.

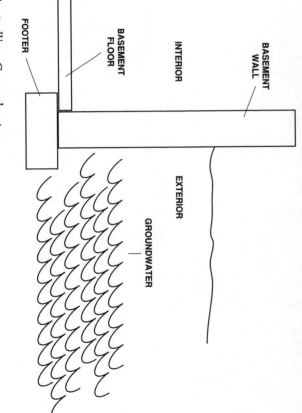

BASEMENT WALL

INTERIOR

EXTERIOR

GROUNDWATER

BASEMENT FLOOR

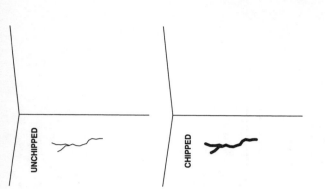

UNCHIPPED

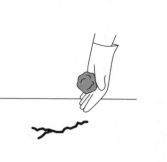

CHIPPED

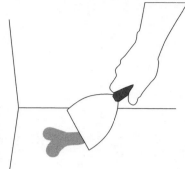

First, prepare the crack or hole by removing any efflorescence from around the area of the crack or hole that needs to be repaired. Efflorescence is a chalky white mineral deposit that is left by water when it passes through concrete. This will also help you identify where the foundation is leaking, since efflorescence needs dampness to form.

Scrape all the efflorescence off the repair area with the stiff wire brush. This project can be dusty, with debris flying around, so make sure you always have on your safety glasses, gloves, and mask.

Once the area is cleaned, you need to prepare the crack or hole by chipping it out and making it larger in order to give the hydraulic cement an edge to bite into and lock onto. Cracks should be chipped out to at least three-quarters of an inch deep and wide. After the crack or hole is chipped out, scrape it down again with the wire brush to remove any loose material.

Before mixing up the hydraulic cement as per the manufacturer's instructions, wet the crack down with some water. This will promote capillary action to help the hydraulic cement stick to the existing concrete. Hydraulic cement also expands as it cures, locking itself into place.

With the concrete wall prepped, mix up the hydraulic cement to the consistency of putty. Roll the cement into a meatball-size shape and firmly press it into the entire crack or hole, leaving plenty of excess hydraulic cement around the repair area. Work fast, because hydraulic cement will start to cure in a matter of minutes. It will also cure underwater, so even if some water is seeping out of the crack, it will still work!

Once the crack or hole is filled, you need to scrape off the excess hydraulic cement with your trowel before it becomes rock hard. As you scrape off the extra cement, push toward the crack or hole. Finally, brush the surface lightly to blend it in, and you're done!

Waterproofing the Walls and Floor: When all the concrete cracks and holes are sealed, water entering your basement will be reduced, but you're not out of the woods yet. Although hard and strong, concrete is a very porous material and groundwater may still work its way through the basement walls and floor. The solution is to waterproof the concrete.

Damp-proofing is one thing, but waterproofing is completely different. A waterproof coating applied to foundation walls and floors will seal up the porous concrete and offer protection against water under pressure. Groundwater is considered water under pressure.

There are two types of waterproof foundation coatings available, the new paint type sold ready to go in one-gallon buckets and the old-school heavy, dry, powder cement type that you have to mix up yourself with water and apply it as a skim coat to the concrete.

Both form a strong mechanical bond with concrete to create a waterproof seal. Cement powder coatings do cost less, and some contractors prefer them over paints, because skim coatings can be applied to wet walls. But, because the paint is ready to go and easier to use, you may want to use the paint-type coating. Here's how to apply it:

Tools and Materials Needed: A stiff wire brush, a stiff and heavy paintbrush, safety glasses, gloves, paint respirator mask, heavy-duty paint roller, and rags. Along with the concrete waterproofing paint for the walls, have enough of the floor-type paint as well.

Apply the waterproof paint per the manufacturer's instructions. My tips are to work the paint into the walls with the stiff brush and use the roller for the floor coat. As in regular painting, surface preparation is the key. Wash and remove any stains, efflorescence, mildew, and so on. Also have all the concrete patching and repairs completed and let the walls and floor dry out completely.

Don't forget to wear your safety gear, turn off fuel-based heating equipment, and have plenty of ventilation when painting. Once the waterproof paint dries, you'll notice that your basement will feel dry as well!

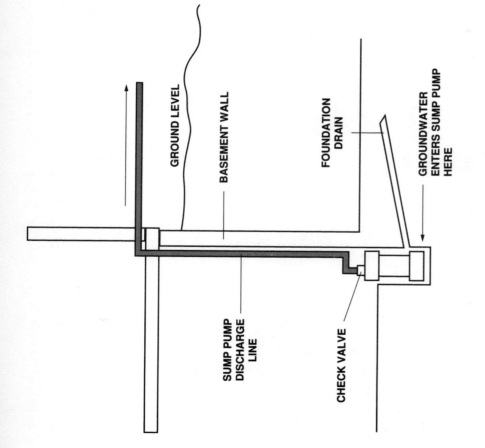

GROUND LEVEL

BASEMENT WALL

FOUNDATION DRAIN

GROUNDWATER ENTERS SUMP PUMP HERE

SUMP PUMP DISCHARGE LINE

CHECK VALVE

Sumps and Pumps: Some wet basements may only need patching and waterproofing of the foundation to stay dry. But there are a lot of basements built in very wet areas that require additional measures to help control the groundwater. This is called a *sump system.*

Most basements built in wet areas or where groundwater is present should have a square pit in a corner of the floor, called a *sump pit.* This is where the below-grade house drains, or *French drains,* distribute the underground water. The sump is the low spot where all the water under a house collects to prevent basement flooding.

The water level in most sumps will rise and fall depending on the amount of rain an area receives. Other sump pits can actually stay full of water all the time due to a high groundwater table.

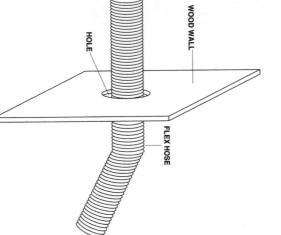

WOOD WALL

HOLE

FLEX HOSE

TROUBLE NOTE

A sump pump will not stop groundwater. A sump pump is a measure for controlling and diverting water away from your basement. If you live on a high water table with groundwater constantly running through your basement, be aware that even with a sump pump installed, pump or power failures can still cause basement flooding to occur.

Sumps often will have an overflow gravity drain line to carry the rising water out of the basement before it floods. But with many sumps, a gravity drain is not possible because of the lay of the land. In that case a *sump pump* needs to be installed to protect the basement from flooding.

A sump pump sits in the sump pit. It has an electrical float switch. When the water rises in the sump, the float switch turns on the pump and the pump pulls the rising water out of the sump pit and pushes it through a drain line that's piped to the outside of the house.

Many sump pumps come complete with the necessary check valves and wiring built into the unit, and most will have standard electrical plugs for the power supply. Many areas may require a permit for this job, and you'll need to have an approved electrical outlet installed by a licensed electrician. Also, connection of the sump pump's drain line into a house's sewer system is usually not allowed. Check your local codes first!

The trick to easily installing a sump pump is to purchase a ready-to-go pump prewired and complete with a check valve built in. You also want a connection on the pump that will accept flexible coiled drain piping. This will allow you to run a drain line uninterrupted to the outdoors without installing any additional fittings.

Contractors usually will run ridged PVC drain piping using "glue and screw" fittings and a remote check valve in the piping. If you are comfortable with and know how to install

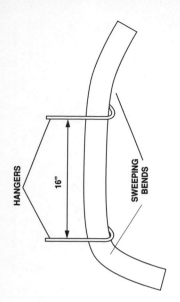

HANGERS

16"

SWEEPING
BENDS

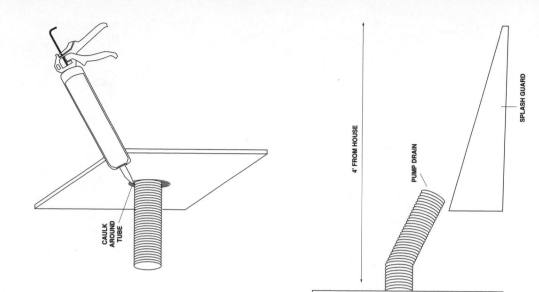

CAULK
AROUND
TUBE

4' FROM HOUSE

PUMP DRAIN

SPLASH GUARD

a PVC drain system, you can purchase a professional-model pump and install the sump pump from scratch according to the manufacturer's instructions.

Tools and Materials Needed: Along with a submersible sump pump, built-in check valve, and flexible piping kit, you'll need your hand tool kit with a plastic pipe cutter, pipe hangers, clamps, wire ties, drill with hole-saw bit, silicone sealer, gutter splash guard, and concrete patio block.

Follow the manufacturer's instructions per your pump. The usual first step for installing a sump pump into a sump is to prepare the pit for the pump. At the bottom of most sumps there should be crushed stone; others may have a plastic bucket-type pit. Either way, you want to lay down a concrete patio block to give the pump a firm base to sit on.

Stretch out your coil of flexible plastic drainpipe, making sure you have more than enough to reach outside the house. You want the discharge line to exit the house close by the pump area. Find a location where you can easily drill a hole through a wooden wall or plate.

Usually the hole will have to be an inch and a half in diameter to fit the drain piping. If you're uncomfortable about drilling big holes or if you have to go through concrete, you should consult a professional.

Connect the flexible piping to the pump's discharge fitting with a stainless-

PRO TIP

If your sump is full of water, the pump should run and you can test the drain and water discharge. If your sump is dry, you may have to wait for the first rainstorm to test your pump. I would not recommend doing any remodeling of the basement until you test the pump.

---

steel clamp and place the sump pump on the concrete block. Check that the pump has plenty of room around its float switch. Some pumps may have a built-in float switch. Stretch the electrical cord out and away from the sump pit, making sure to keep it unplugged for now.

Once you have the pump in place and the hole drilled to the outside of the house, it's time to run and hang the flexible drain piping. Remember, flexible drains are soft and need extra support, with more pipe hangers than ridged piping. You want to avoid low spots.

Run the drain line vertically, up from the pump until you reach the first pipe hanger off the ceiling, and then bend it toward the hole in the wall, making sure you don't kink the drain line. Continue to run and hang the drain and push plenty of piping through the hole to the exterior of the house.

Go outside and make sure the pipe runs in a continuous downward pitch to reduce the chances of freezing up in the winter. Once the pipe is secured and in place on the ground, seal up around the hole in the house with the silicone caulking. Place the splash guard under the end of the drain, making sure the water drains at least four feet away from the house.

With the pump and drain installed and the approved electrical outlet in place, you can now finish the job. Make sure your electrician has complied with your local electrical codes. Since the pump sits in water, most areas may require that the outlet be a ground fault circuit interrupter outlet. The last step is to plug in the pump.

Dehumidifiers: To maintain dryness in the basement, the most useful appliance you can install is a dehumidifier. A dehumidifier uses a supercooled coil to condense the moist air and draw out the water. The water will collect in a bucket that you empty when it's full. Dehumidifiers are also great for crawl spaces.

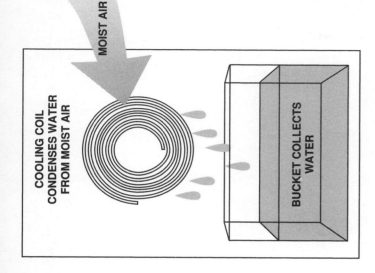

MOIST AIR

COOLING COIL
CONDENSES WATER
FROM MOIST AIR

BUCKET COLLECTS
WATER

If you have a sump, you can let the dehumidifier drain directly into the pit, which will avoid the need to empty the collection bucket. Dehumidifiers also have a humidistat built in so you can control the moisture levels in your basement. Now you know all about the "Three G's"!

We all know the saying "Start from the bottom and work your way up!" Well, this applies perfectly to how you should tackle projects around your house. Starting at the bottom is a great way to introduce yourself to the world of home improvement. The basement is an area of your home that usually requires immediate attention and very little skill is needed to complete most of the basement projects that I mentioned. So if you're ready to become the master of your domain, my advice is to start in your basement and then work your way up to the other spaces and places in your home that need attention.

CONTRACTORS AND BIG PROJECTS

Ed's worlds of wisdom on contractors and homeowners: *"When communicating with a contractor about your home, there are usually two sides to every story of the house. Listening to each other is the key to a successful project.*

No matter what your skill level is or how many tools you own, eventually a home-improvement project will come along that will require some outside help. For some it may be a small project like changing a shower's mixing valve. More experienced homeowners may not need outside help until it's time to remodel the kitchen. Bottom line is that we all, even contractors, have limitations on what we can do alone.

If you want to keep out of trouble, know your limits and know when you may be pushing yourself too hard, both physically and mentally. There's an old saying that a lawyer "never asks a question without knowing the answer before hand." That's the same thinking you need to keep in mind with home improvement. If you don't know all the answers to potential problems that may arise, don't attempt the project alone!

That said, once you do bring in an outside contractor, there's now a new set of rules you have to play by. When you work alone, you can usually visualize exactly what you want, and the process of bringing those ideas to fruition can be a very rewarding experience. Just look at fine woodworkers or craftspeople who love working by themselves with blocks of wood and methodically bringing a piece of furniture to life.

When you introduce another person into this mix, especially if it's a contractor who possesses more building skills than you, it may be intimidating to convey your ideas to that person. The difference between a successful relationship with your contractor and an unsuccessful one is the ability to communicate clearly with each other.

But first you have to find the right contractor for the job. A reporter once asked me, "How can you find the best contractor in your area?" I thought for a moment, and when the answer hit me, it made surprising sense. I said, "You should not necessarily look for the best contractor. Look for the contractor who's best for you."

FINDING "YOUR" BEST CONTRACTOR

Start with a List of Names

Finding a good contractor is kind of like being a private eye looking for a missing person. Get in touch with the people who are most likely to give you the information you need. Contact the local building-supply houses, town inspectors, and friends of yours who've had some remodeling work done recently to get recommendations you can trust.

A bad contractor will leave a trail of destruction and pending lawsuits. But a good contractor—someone who pays bills on time to the supply house, has a good reputation with local inspectors, and is known to customers for doing quality work—will build a positive reputation across the board. The trick is to find a name or names that pop up more than once. Keep asking around, and eventually you'll have a list of several reputable contractors.

Research Your Project

Once you have a few solid leads, you now have to do some research on your project before you set up any meetings. A good contractor enjoys working with an educated customer who understands the scope of the job. Remember, this is a two-way street. To get a good contractor for your job, you need to create a professional and comfortable working environment from the start, so that the contractor will want to do your work. Your goal is to get the contractor excited about your job!

Thorough research involves gathering information about the types of materials you want to use for the project and a reasonable timeline for the work. You will also need to develop a strategy in advance for coping with and living around the construction. For example, if you're doing a major remodeling job on your only bathroom with a tub and shower, let the contractor know you've already made other living arrangements for the period when your main bathroom will be shut down. Information like this goes a long way with contractors, because they know that you've already thought through the entire project.

Here are some other issues you should do a little research on before meeting with potential contractors:

- The *Impact on your neighbors and neighborhood*—Where will the contractor and subcontractors park all their vehicles? What about noise and disruption to your neighbors' lifestyle? Believe it or not, most of the problems that I have seen with large remodeling jobs and trouble with the town regulations and inspectors have come from a trusted neighbor calling the inspectors with complaints about a job!

- *Your budget limitations*—When you do a project, you need to know how much cash you have on hand and the limit you can borrow from the bank. Decide that that's your budget and you will not go over it, no matter how tempting! Keep reminding your contractor of your budget—a good contractor will feel more comfortable with clients who set and stay within their limits than with clients who commit to spending an amount they can't afford. Remember, a contractor wants to be paid in full and will work with you to stay in budget.

- *Licenses, permits, and insurance*—You need to find out what your area and state require a local contractor to carry for licenses and/or registrations in order to do work in your home. Whatever the minimum requirements, you should see proof of this license and/or registration from your contractor. Proof of insurance is required as well in many areas in order to take out permits for building and remodeling projects.

- *Your contractor's subcontractors*—On a major project, just about all contractors will work with subcontractors. You need to know the local regulations regarding subcontractors on your job. Find out if the sub needs to show proof of licenses and insurance as well. Good contractors and subs know all the local rules and will cooperate with you.

- *Availability to make decisions*—You may have a contractor working on your job, but don't lose sight of the fact that the contractor is working for you! A good contractor knows that issues may come up that will require your timely approval to keep the project on schedule. Do some communication research and have a plan in place so that the contractor can contact you quickly about major decisions for the project.

Getting the Bid

The purpose of the first meeting with a contractor is not only to get a feel of how you can communicate with a potential contractor but also to see if the contractor can bid the work within your budget.

I recommend having a least two contractors, but no more than four, bid on the job. The local contracting community is usually very small, and if word gets around that you're meeting with everyone in town, it may work against you. Contractors may perceive a person calling many builders as someone out shopping for the lowest price.

The first thing you need to discuss is the plan and scope of the work. Some contractors may want to include a complete floor plan or blueprint in their price, or you may have the plan already drawn up for the contractor's review. Either way, remember that the more detailed the plan, the less likely it is that a discrepancy will occur between you and the contractor.

Smaller contracting jobs like service calls or repairs may be priced at *cost plus*. This is where you will agree on an hourly rate and then the contractor will bill you for time and materials. Cost plus does move things along quickly, but it's very important for you and the contractor to keep in constant communication regarding the current job costs.

Larger remodeling or building projects should be *fixed price* to protect everyone's best interests. This is when the contractor will give one price per the blueprint for the complete job, including labor and materials. Any changes or extra work outside the scope of the plan is usually charged at a cost-plus rate. Many jobs end up a combination of fixed price and cost plus.

PRO TIP

Consult an architect. I have always viewed professional blueprints as the best contract between a homeowner and a contractor. With detailed blueprints everything is right there in black and white (well, blue and white) for everyone to follow!

Compare All Bids

When comparing and choosing between contractor bids, never go on price alone. Always look at the entire bid package, the reputation of the contractor, and your gut feelings about working with the particular person. Trust me on this one. Think of this potential relationship like a marriage:

- Can you live with this person in your house every day?

- Do you communicate very well with this person?

- Will this person spend all your money carefully?

- How will this person treat your children?

- When will this person finally leave? (Time frame is important!)

And *most* important, can this person do the job you're asking for? Usually, with a few contractors bidding on the job, one of them should meet all the standards you set up for the job.

Even if the price is a little higher, you'll probably be better off paying a bit more rather than agreeing to work with someone you're not sure about.

TROUBLE NOTE

I always say that if a contractor has nothing else to offer except a cheap price, all you'll get is a cheap job!

BUYER BEWARE

One thing about being a contractor for a while is that you get to know many other contractors, both good and not so good. I've noticed that some questionable contractors do share many bad habits. Remember, I'm not saying that if contractors do one or all of these things, they're not good contractors. I just want to list a few warning signs of what's known in the business as a "fly-by-night contractor":

- Quotes prices that always seem unbelievably low.

- Drives an unmarked truck or car in poor repair.

- Goes door-to-door with a high-pressure sales pitch.

- Will not show current licenses or insurances.

- Is reluctant to take out permits for the project.

Consider any of these behaviors warning signs when reviewing potential contractors.

CLOSING THE DEAL

Okay. So far you've looked around, done some research, and finally found a contractor you want to work with who wants to work with you. Sounds like you're ready to start the job!

Sorry, not yet. There's one more thing to take care of, and that is a final contract between you and your contractor. Many homeowners and contractors will get to this point and then drop the ball. At this stage you might be thinking, "I really like this contractor. Nothing can go wrong. We don't have to waste time on a contract!" And the builder might agree.

Bad move! I've been there and done that, and it rarely works out. It's the contract that will protect your good relationship. Memories are short, especially when it comes to money. A contract between two parties who like each other is a reminder of exactly what both of you agreed on at the beginning of the job. The promises are in writing, so that will help head off a conflict that can occur down the road, even if you are friends with your contractor.

Once a project begins, it's easy to go back and forth about missing items or something being charged as an extra when it should have been included. Both parties may feel that they are right and they're the ones losing out and getting the short end of the stick. This is the start of a relationship falling apart. A contract is a clear-cut reminder to one person that he or she may be forgetting something that was promised.

But as good as a contract is, it's usually not a be-all and end-all document. I have been in a few frustrating situations where a person or business has flat-out broken a contracted promise with me, and sometimes the best option is to sit back and take it. But in most cases a good contract between honest, well-meaning individuals is a very valuable asset to getting the job done without any major disagreements. Bottom line is this old saying: "Get it in writing!"

ED'S TEN THINGS
TO CONSIDER WHEN SIGNING A CONTRACT

1. Contact a lawyer before you sign the contract, just to cover your bases.

2. If you have a good blueprint, incorporate mentions of it into the contract (i.e., "as per approved plans or blueprints").

3. Include the starting date of the work and "finish-by" completion dates.

4. Include a detailed description of the project, the brand names and/or grades of materials to be used, and who supplies what materials.

5. Indicate who will pay for any government fees, taxes, and/or permits.

6. Include the total agreed price of the main project, a payment schedule, and how extra work or job changes will be invoiced and paid for.

7. Clearly state who will pay for extra equipment like cranes, delivery trucks, or Dumpsters and who is responsible for keeping the job site clean.

8. Clarify material and labor warranties. Spell this out completely, especially if the homeowner is supplying any materials or fixtures.

9. Clearly state who pays the subcontractors for extra work, whose insurance the subs will work under, and a copy of the contractor's insurance.

10. Finally, make sure both parties sign the contract!

Remember, this is just a quick rundown of some topics that should be written into the contract. Along with your contractor, you may want to add other details, like any special promises or free extras that will be thrown into the job by the contractor.

Also, if you will be working on some aspect of the job with the contractor to save a little money, write out your exact duties and the time frame in which you will complete these tasks for the contractor. In this case the contractor will be protected if you fail to comply with your duties.

ED'S TEN-STEP PROJECT-COMPLETION PROCESS

The end of one journey is over—you've made it to the point where you and your contractor are ready to start the job. Sorry, but this just means another new journey is about to begin—that is, completing the whole process.

To help you navigate through all the joys and stresses of doing a major home-improvement project, I put together this step-by-step list, complete with all the "official" contractor lingo:

1. The blueprints and contracts are "executed" and signed.

2. All building permits have been "pulled" from the city or town.

3. Any "demo" work or "gutting" needed has been started and completed.

4. Contractor starts "rough" carpentry and framing work.

5. Subs install all "rough" plumbing, electrical, HVAC, and so on.

6. Town or city inspectors give the "green tag" for "rough" work approval

7. Subs "hang" and "mud" drywall for walls and ceiling.

8. Contractor and subs install the "finish" work and materials.

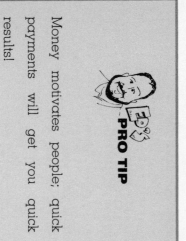

PRO TIP

Money motivates people; quick payments will get you quick results!

9. Building inspector returns for "final" inspection and "green tags."

10. Contractor and homeowner complete "walk-through" and final payment.

This is a basic guide to follow, although you may need to tweak a few steps along the way. I recommend you post my list and make it a checklist for everyone to keep track of together. Check off and date every completed step. You'll be surprised how much smoother a job can run when everyone is reminded about how the job is progressing.

HOMESCHOOLED

If and when you need to hire a contractor, don't think of it as "spending" money. From now on, I want you to think of it as an in "investment" in your home and in yourself!

If you work closely with your contractor on larger projects around your house, it will be like going to home-improvement school. Before you know it, you'll have the confidence to tackle more and more projects around your house, by yourself.

For example, a friend of mine named Bob is a lawyer who enjoyed working on his home. He's also pretty smart, because he figured out the secret of doing large home-improvement projects on his own.

The secret is learning something new from every contracted job that takes place in your home. Bob has worked closely with all his contractors and picked up a lot of valuable information over the years. Plus, Bob and I share the same positive theory of success. It's the old saying, "What one person can do, so can another." All it takes is time.

Confident thinking like that will allow you to go after new challenges that you never thought possible! Bob took all the skills he learned from working with his contractors, plus the confidence he had in himself, and crossed over into the blue-collar contracting world.

Today Bob is one of the best all-around home-improvement experts I know. Some of his beautifully completed home projects: installing hardwood floors throughout his home, turning an extra bedroom into a designer bathroom, gutting a living room and turning it into a huge formal dining room complete with old-fashioned tin ceilings, building a cedar-plank fence from scratch around his pool, and turning his basement into a workshop so he can do all these wonderful projects.

The quality of his work rivals that of the contractors he learned from—not bad for a lawyer with no previous building experience. Remember, what one person can do, so can another. Now get to work!

HOME-REPAIR LINGO

Whether it's a medical book or a home-improvement book, sometimes the words can get confusing. Naturally, if you don't understand what a word means, you're not going to learn about the subject. Many times even *with* a glossary, the explanation can be tougher to understand than the word itself!

In my glossary I've included the most popular words I've heard used in the home-improvement field, and my explanations don't come from a dictionary or a manual. These are my interpretations of the words and terms that have served me well over my thirty-plus years in the home-building field. If they worked for me, they'll work for you! I've also included the category of construction this term would most likely be used in, to help you understand the meanings and learn the differences between words that may sound alike.

Access panel—(General construction) A removable panel for accessing system controls behind walls, ceilings, or floors that need to be serviced.

Adapters—(Plumbing) Male or female threaded transition fittings that adapt threaded ends to soldered or glued joints or can join different types of pipe.

Aerator—(Plumbing) Screw-in control found at the end of most sink faucet spouts to restrict the water flow and introduce air into the water to soften the flow.

Aggregate—(General construction) Smaller-size crushed rock or gravel. Used as a fill material, and it's also one of the main ingredients in concrete.

Amp—(Electrical) One of the standard measurements of electrical current in a circuit. Common use of the term is for sizing circuit breakers and fuses.

Auger—(Plumbing) Flexible metal coiled, snakelike cable used for clearing clogs in drain lines. Spins as it travels and is powered by hand or motor.

Ballast—(Electrical) Transformer found in fluorescent light fixtures that sets the light up with proper voltage. Commonly confused with *baluster*.

Baluster—(Carpentry) Spindles spaced close together in staircase rails that support the rail and add beauty and safety. Commonly confused with *ballast*.

Bat—(Masonry) A full brick broken into two equal pieces will create two bats. A bat is used to fill a space where a full brick is too large to fit.

Batt—(General construction) Nothing to do with bricks! It's a standard section of fiberglass insulation measuring in range from fifteen inches wide to eight feet long.

Batten—(Carpentry) Nothing to do with bricks or insulation! It's a small, thin strip of wood used to cover seams between larger wood panels or boards.

Beam—(Carpentry) Horizontal timber or steel support that spans a gap and supports the roof or floor joists above. Used when a bearing wall is absent.

Bearing wall—(Carpentry) Interior or exterior wall that supports the roof or floor joists above. Cannot be removed unless replaced with a support beam.

Bevel cut—(General construction) A cut made on a piece of wood, metal, stone, or any building materials other than a ninety-degree angle. A tapered cut.

Bimetal—(Electrical) Part of a switch composed of two ("bi") metals that heat and cool at different rates to close or open a circuit. Used in thermostats.

Blind nail—(Carpentry) Used for finish woodwork to hide the nail heads so they cannot be seen. Finish nails and wood putty are used for this effect.

BTU / British thermal unit—(Plumbing) Rating system for any heating equipment. Amount of energy needed to raise one pound of water one degree Fahrenheit.

Bullnose—(General construction) Finish materials with a rounded exposed end, to taper the look or make a transition. Use on the last course of wall tiles and the like.

Butt joint—(General construction) A joint created between two pieces of material by butting them together on a ninety-degree angle. No angle cuts.

Cantilever—(General construction) Joists or beams that overhang and project beyond a supporting member of the construction frame.

Capillary action—(General construction) Occurs when a liquid is drawn into thin spaces or around objects like wire and follows the material for a distance.

Cement—(Masonry) Cement is not concrete. It is the processed powder that serves as the binding material in concrete and gives it its strength and bonding power.

Cement board—(Masonry) Similar to drywall, but it's made for wet walls such as those enclosing showers or bathtubs. Tile is applied directly to cement board.

Certificate of occupancy—(General construction) This certificate is issued by the municipality upon inspection and is required to occupy a dwelling. Often called a C of O or C/O.

CFM—(Electrical) Cubic feet per minute that an electrical fan can move.

Clean-out—(Plumbing) A removable threaded access plug in plumbing drain lines.

Conduit—(Electrical) Pipelike sleeve that electrical wires run through.

Counterbore—(Carpentry) To drive a nail or screw below the surface.

Countersink—(Carpentry) To drive a nail or screw flush with the surface of any material.

Crosscut—(Carpentry) To cut a piece of lumber across the grain.

Damper—(Plumbing/HVAC) A baffle inside a flue or duct with a lever on the outside of the flue or duct to control the system's airflow.

DWV—(Plumbing) Drain, waste, vent system. The complete network of the venting and drainage system carrying wastewater from a dwelling or building.

Drywall—(General construction) Actual name of gypsum board commonly hung for wall and ceiling materials. Sheetrock is a brand name commonly used.

Dry wall—(Masonry) Stone or block wall using no concrete or mortar.

Efflorescence—(Masonry) White, powdery stains on concrete walls or floors caused by salts and minerals leaching out of the concrete itself due to moisture issues.

Elbow—(Plumbing) Any type of pipe fitting that changes direction ninety degrees.

End grain—(Carpentry) Cut section of exposed wood grain on a board.

Expansion joint—(General construction) Mechanical joint on a system or materials made to absorb expansion and contraction of the material due to heating and cooling.

Extras—(General construction) Extra work not covered in a contract.

Fall—(Plumbing) Also called pitch, refers to downward drain slope.

Fascia board—(Carpentry) Long horizontal board used to finish off rafter ends.

Female—(Plumbing) Any internal fitting accepting an external male fitting end.

Filler—(General construction) Caulking or wood putty used to fill gaps.

Finish Work—(General construction) The process of installing wood trim, fixtures, tile, or any other materials to complete the job.

Fish—(Electrical) To pull wires through the inside of finished walls. The snaking tool used has a hook on the end to "catch" the wire.

Fixture drains—(Plumbing) The smaller branch drains off a main drain.

Flux—(Plumbing) A mild chemical gel used to draw solder into a copper pipe joint.

Footing—(General construction) A heavy concrete supporting base installed below the frost line, designed to carry heavy loads.

Furring—(Carpentry) Inexpensive, rough wood strips used for support.

Galvanized metals—(General construction) Metals coated with zinc to help protect them from rust and wear due to exposure or moisture.

GFCI—(Electrical) Ground fault circuit interrupter, used anywhere water can come in contact with an outlet. Automatically shuts down a circuit.

Green board—(General construction) Used in wet areas such as tub or shower walls in place of drywall.

Gusset—(Carpentry) Cool name for a wood support and cover board installed over a joint.

Header—(Carpentry) Heavy, strong horizontal wood support spanning an approved gap such as a door or window to hold the weight above.

Hot wire—(Electrical) The wire carrying electrical current to a receptacle.

HVAC—(Plumbing/HVAC) Stands for heating, venting, air-conditioning systems.

Increaser—(Plumbing) Fitting used to join smaller pipes to larger pipes.

Jack studs—(Carpentry) Studs used to support headers on either side.

Joists—(Carpentry) Horizontal framing supports for floors and ceilings.

Knockouts—(General construction) Factory-installed tabs that can be knocked out of materials with a hammer to create an opening or pass-through.

Lag bolt—(General construction) Thick, heavy-duty hex head bolt.

Lag screw—(General construction) Thick, heavy-duty hex head screw used in wood or shields.

Laminate—(Carpentry) Generic term for the hard plastic veneer used for countertops. The popular brand name is Formica.

Lap joint—(Carpentry) A joint created when one piece of building material laps over another.

Load bearing—(Carpentry) Refers to a wall or beam that is key in supporting a structure and should not be tampered with or removed.

MDF—(Carpentry) Medium-density fiberboard, made from wood flakes and resins.

Membrane—(General construction) A water-resistant layer on top of or between two materials. Can be found in bathroom walls, exterior walls, and roofs.

Miter joint—(Carpentry) Usually found on finish work. It's the process of joining two pieces of wood or materials cut at the same angle.

NEC—(Electrical) National Electrical Code for safe wiring standards.

Neutral wire—(Electrical) Wire carrying electrical current to the ground. Usually a white wire.

Nipple—(Plumbing) Short run of hard piping with threads on both sides. Available in many sizes.

O ring—(Plumbing) Round-edged rubber rings used to seal components to prevent leaks.

On center—(General construction) Distance between center points of framing members or materials. Can also be the center point of a wall stud.

Overload—(Electrical) Condition that results when a circuit carries more amperage than its rating.

Partition wall—(Carpentry) A non-load-bearing and nonsupporting wall.

PEX—(Plumbing) Polyethylene cross-linked flexible water piping.

Pilot hole—(General construction) Small hole used to create a passageway or locate obstructions.

Plumb—(General construction) Describes a true vertical member on a structure. A plumb bob tool can be used to check this condition.

Primer—(General construction) A heavy first coat of paint to prep a surface for the finish coat.

Prime—(Plumbing) To remove all the air from a system or piping loop.

psi—(Plumbing) Water pressure is rated in pounds per square inch.

Punch list—(General construction) Problem list for the contractor.

PVC—(Plumbing) Polyvinyl chloride plastic drain line piping.

R value—(General construction) Insulation ratings of a material, the higher the R-value number, the better the insulating properties.

Rabbet—(Carpentry) Often mistakenly spelled "rabbit," a notched cut that runs down the edge of a length of wood used to join two pieces.

Rafters—(Carpentry) The parallel framing supports for a roof.

Rebar—(Masonry) Steel reinforcing rods that concrete is poured around until the rods are embedded.

Reducer—(Plumbing) Fitting used to join larger pipes to smaller pipes.

Relief valve—(Plumbing) Automatic opening valve for discharging excessive pressure.

Ridge board—(Carpentry) Top beam at a roof's peak that ties in the roof rafters.

Rip—(Carpentry) To cut boards down the length of the grain.

Rough work—(General construction) The first stages of construction.

Saddle valve—(Plumbing) A mechanical valve used to tap into a water line. Not accepted by all codes.

Scratch coat—(General construction) First or "rough" coat of plaster.

Sheathing—(Carpentry) First sheet of wood coverings over studs and rafters. Can also be the finish cover.

Short circuit—(Electrical) The condition that results when hot and neutral wires make contact.

Sill cock—(Plumbing) The correct term for an outdoor water faucet.

Sleepers—(Carpentry) Boards used for support laid on top of concrete.

Soil stack—(Plumbing) A main vertical drainpipe for carrying waste.

Spalling—(Masonry) Any cracking, chipping, or flaking of concrete.

Stop order—(General construction) You never want to see one of these.

Stop valve—(Plumbing) Isolating valve located at the fixture itself.

Subfloor—(Carpentry) First or rough floor directly above the joists.

Three-four-five—(General construction) This is a formula to check if a corner is square. Measure three feet from the corner in one direction and four feet in the opposite direction. The diagonal distance between the points should be five feet.

Toe kick—(Carpentry) The hollow space between the floor and the bottom of a cabinet. Often "toe-kick heaters" are installed in this area.

Toenail—(Carpentry) To drive a nail in at an angle on a stud or joist.

UL—(General construction) Underwriters Laboratories, a testing agency for electrical equipment.

UPC—(Uniform Plumbing Code) National plumbing system guidelines. Local codes may vary.

Vent stack—(Plumbing) Uppermost portion of a plumbing drainage system passing through the roof to vent the sewer gases.

Voltage—(Electrical) Measurement of electrical power or current flowing in a circuit.

Warped—(Carpentry) Describes bad lumber that has twisted and is unusable for building.

Water hammer—(Plumbing) A sound of banging in the pipes when water is turned on and off suddenly. Usually associated with high water pressure.

Wet wall—(Plumbing) Interior wall containing water and drain lines.

Yard of concrete—(Masonry) One cubic yard of concrete is three feet by three feet by three feet, and one yard of concrete will pour eighty square feet at depth of three and a half inches.

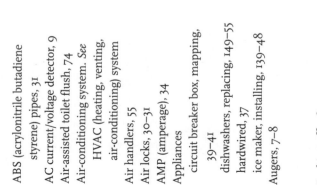

INDEX

ABS (acrylonitrile butadiene styrene) pipes, 31
AC current/voltage detector, 9
Air-assisted toilet flush, 74
Air-conditioning system. *See* HVAC (heating, venting, air-conditioning) system
Air handlers, 55
Air locks, 30–31
AMP (amperage), 34
Appliances
circuit breaker box, mapping, 39–41
dishwashers, replacing, 149–55
hardwired, 37
ice maker, installing, 139–48
Augers, 7–8

Backing off, 98–99
Ballcock, replacing, 76
Baseboard
installing, 183–84
for laminate floor, 169–71
Baseboard radiation, hydronic heat, 53–54

Basement, drying out, 186–97
cracks, repairing, 190–92
dampness, locating source, 186–88
dehumidifiers, 196–97
grading issues, 189
groundwater issues, 190
gutters, repairing, 188–89
sump system, 193–96
walls/floor waterproofing, 192
Basin cock wrenches, 7
Basket strainers, kitchen sink, installing, 135–36
Bathroom
clogged drains. *See* Bathroom clogs; Lavatory clogs
exhaust fans, 108–14
faucets. *See* Lavatory faucets
grab bars, 104–8
lavatory, 86–88
showerheads, 97–104
toilets, 73–86
Bathroom clogs
bathtub/shower drains, 68–72
lavatory, 62–63
toilets, 66–68

Bathtub drains, clearing, 68–72
cylindrical type, 70
hair, cautions about, 69, 72
pop-up stopper type, 70
tub shoe overflow, 70–71
Beadboard. *See* Wainscoting
Bids, from contractors, 202–4
Boilers, compared with furnaces, 51–52
Branch lines, 30
Brass pipes, 29
Breakers. *See* Circuit breaker boxes
BTUs (British thermal units), 46–47
Bus bars, 36
Butt joints, baseboard installation, 171, 183–84
BX cable, 45

Cap plungers, 8
Carpentry, tools for, 9–10
Cast-iron, pipes, 32
sinks, 132–33
Cement, hydraulic, 190–91

CFMs (cubic feet per minute), 113

Chair rails, rabbet cuts, 184–85

Chalk line, 5

Circuit breaker boxes, 34–42
and appliance installation, 152
double toggle switch, 40
functions of, 34
GFCI breakers, 38
grounded system, 38–39
layout, 37–38
and light fixture installation, 172
main shutoff, 36
mapping circuits of house, 39–41
operation of, 36–38
resetting, 41–42
tripping breaker, 34, 36, 41–42
voltages, 36

Circular saws, 9

Circulator pump, hydronic heat, 53–54

Clogged drains. *See* Bathroom clogs; Kitchen sink clogs; Lavatory clogs

Closet augers, 7, 67–68

Combination squares, 10

Contractors, 200–209
bidding by, 202–4
cautions about, 204
client information needs, 201–2
contract with, 206–7
project completion list, 207–8

Contracts, with contractors, 206–7

Copper, drainpipes, 32

tubing, water line, 143

Cordless tools, 5, 9–11

Countertops, 138–39
material options, 139

CPVC (chlorinated polyvinyl chloride) pipes, 28

Crawl space, 185

Dehumidifiers, drying basement, 196–97

Dishwashers, 149–55
new, installing, 152–55
old, removing, 150–52
replacement criteria, 149

Diverter valve, 102

Drain augers, 8, 64–65

Drain system, 29–30

Drains, clogged. *See* Bathroom clogs; Kitchen sink clogs; Lavatory clogs

Drills, recommended type, 5

Drop-in lavatory, 86

Drywall repair, 161–65
damage, forms of, 161
gouges and cracks, 162–63
holes, 163–65

Duct systems, air-based heating/cooling, 54–55

Efflorescence, 191

Eighteen-gauge wire, 45

Electrical system, 33–46
AMP (amperage), 34
electrical wire, types of, 45
electric meter, 33
GFCI (ground fault circuit interrupters), 38, 44–45
grounded system, 38–39
main power shutoff, 33–34
service (hot) wires, 34
See also Circuit breaker boxes; Fuse-type electrical systems

Electrical work, tools for, 9

Electric hammer drill, 11

Electric heat, 48

Engineered-material countertops, 139

Exhaust fans, 108–14
CFMs (cubic feet per minute), 113
functions of, 109
maintenance of, 109–11

Faucets. *See* Kitchen sink faucets; Lavatory faucets

Firebox, of burners, 52

Fixture isolation, 91

Fixture traps, 30

Flapper, replacing, 78–79

Flexible braided stainless steel, water line, 143–44, 147

Floating floors, *See* Laminate flooring

Flooring, laminate, glueless. *See* Laminate flooring

Force cup plungers, 8, 66, 68, 119

Forced hot-water heat, 53–54

Fourteen-gauge wire, 45

French drains, 193

Furnaces, compared with boilers, 51–52

Fuse-type electrical systems, 34–35
blowing fuse, 34, 42–43
changing fuse, 42–43
updating, 35

Galvanized pipes, 29

Garbage disposers, 117–19
maintenance of, 118–19
reset breaker overload, 117–18

Gas heating
natural gas, 49–50
propane gas, 50

GFCI (ground fault circuit interrupters)
GFCI breakers, 38
purpose of, 38, 44
testing/resetting, 44–45

Grab bars, 104–8
installing, 105–8
placement guidelines, 105

sizing, 112–13

venting system, 112–13

Grabbing tools, 8, 64, 68, 72
Grading, and basement
    dampness, 189
Granite countertops, 139
Gravity toilet flush, 73–74
Grounding, electrical system,
    38–39
Grounding rods, 38
Grounding wires, 38
Groundwater, and basement
    dampness, 190
Gutters, and basement
    dampness, 188–89

Hammer drills, 5, 11
Hardwired appliances, 37
Heat exchangers, 52
Heating system. See HVAC
    (heating, venting, air-
    conditioning) system
Heating zones, 54
Heat pumps, 55
Hole saws, 5
Hot-air heating systems, 54–55
Hot wires, electrical, 34
HVAC (heating, venting, air-
    conditioning) system, 46–56
BTUs (British thermal units),
    46–47
climate/choosing system, 55–56
electric heat, 48
furnace compared with boiler,
    51–52
hot-air heating, 54–55
hydronic heat, 53–54
natural gas heat, 49–50
oil heat, 48–49
propane gas heat, 50
solar energy, 50–51
steam heat, 52–53
thermostat, 47–48
Hydraulic cement, basement
    crack repair, 190–91
Hydronic heat, 53–54

Ice makers. See Refrigerator
    dispensers
Insurance, contractors, 202

Jigsaws, 5, 180

Kitchen
    countertops, 138–39
    dishwashers, replacing, 149–55
    garbage disposers, 117–19
    refrigerator dispensers,
        139–48
    sinks. See Kitchen sink(s)
Kitchen sink(s)
    bowl style, 130–31
    cast-iron, 132–33
    drain clogs. See Kitchen sink
        clogs
    dressing, 135–36
    faucets. See Kitchen sink
        faucets
    new, installing, 135–38
    old, removing, 133–35
    size options, 131–32
    stainless-steel, 132–33
    top/under-mounted, 138
Kitchen sink clogs
    clearing, 118–19
    double-bowl sink, 119
Kitchen sink faucets, 120–30
    deck-mounted, 124–25, 130
    new, installing, 125–30
    old, removing, 121–25
    styles of, 120–21

Laminate countertops, 139
Laminate flooring, 166–71
    laying floor, 167–69
    trim, 169–71
Lavatory, 86–88
    drain clogs. See Lavatory clogs
    faucet holes, 87–88
    faucets. See Lavatory faucets
    types of, 86–87
Lavatory clogs, 62–65
    drain clogs, 64–65
    pop-up assemblies, 63
    trap clogs, 63–64
Lavatory faucets, 89–96
    installing, 93–96
    pop-up assemblies, 92, 94–95
    quick-install type, 89–90
    removing, 90–93
Lead pipes, 32
Levels, 7
Light fixtures, 171–74
    new, installing, 173–74
    old, removing, 171–73
    weight aspects, 171
LPG (liquefied petroleum gas), 50

Main power shutoff, 33–34, 36
Main water feed line, 27
Main water shutoff valve, 26–27
Miter joints, baseboard
    installation, 170–71, 183
Molding
    installing, 184–85
    for laminate floor, 169–70

Natural gas heat, 49–50
Needle valves, 140–41
Neutral wires, electrical, 34
Nonpotable water, 25

Oil burner, 48
Oil heat, 48–49
One-hole lavatory, 87–88

Pedestal sink, 87
Personal shower, 100–104
    arm-mounted installation,
        100–101

Personal shower (cont)
  diverter valve, 102
  styles of, 100
  wall-mounted installation,
    101–4
Phantom flush, 78
Pipes
  drain/vent pipes, 31–32
  water pipes, 28–29
Plastic tubing, water line, 143,
    147
Plumbing, tools for, 7–9
Plumbing system, 24–32
  cold-water line, 25–26
  drain system, 29–30
  drain/vent pipes, types of, 31–32
  hot-water piping, 27
  main water feed line, 27
  main water shutoff valve, 27
  waste vent system, 30–31
  water pipes, types of, 28–29
Plungers. See Cap plungers;
    Force cup plungers
Pop-up assemblies
  clearing clogs, 63, 70
Potable water, 25
Power-assisted toilet flush, 74–75
Power miter saws, 10
Pressure-lite toilet, 74
Propane gas heat, 50
Propane torches, 9
Pullout blocks. See Fuse-type
    electrical systems, 34
Pullout-spray faucet, 121
PVC (polyvinyl chloride) pipes,
    31, 194–95

Quarter-round molding,
  installing, 170
Quick-install faucets, 89–90

PEX (polyethylene cross-linked)
    pipes, 28–29

Rabbet cut, chair rails, 184–85
Radiant heating, 54
Radiators, steam heat, 52–53
Reciprocating saws, 6
Refrigerator dispensers, 139–48
  piping options, 143–44
  supply line, running, 144–45
  tap into water line, 140–42
  water/refrigerator connections,
    145–48
Registers, air-based heating/
    cooling, 54–55
Rentals, tools, 13–14
Right angle drills, 6
Routers, 10

Saddle valves, 140–41
Saws, types of, 10–11
Scarf joint, baseboard installation,
    184
Septic systems, 22–23
  maintaining, 23
Service head, 33
Sewer ejectors, 30
Sewers, public, 21
Sheetrock damage. See Drywall
    repair
Short circuit, tripping breaker, 36
Showerheads, 97–104
  new, installing, 99–100
  old, removing, 98–99
  personal shower, 100–104
  water-saving types, 97
Shower stall drain, clearing, 71–72
Sink clogs. See Kitchen sink
    clogs; Lavatory clogs
Sinks. See Kitchen sink(s);
    Lavatory
Slab foundation, 185
Sledgehammers, 6
Solar energy, 50–51
Stainless-steel sinks, 132–33
Steam heat, 52–53

Studs
  locating, 177–78
  stud finder, 6, 177
Subcontractors, 202, 206
Sump system, installing, 193–96
  cover, 187
Supply tubes, 92

Table saws, 10
Ten-gauge wire, 45
Thermostat, 47–48
Three G's, 187, 188–92
Three-wire NM 3G cable, 45
Thresholds, installing, 170
Tile
  countertops, 139
  cutters, 11
  wall, drilling, 103
  work, tools for, 11
Toilets, 73–86
  air-assisted flush, 74
  ballcock replacement, 76
  clogs, clearing, 66–68
  flapper replacement, 78–79
  gravity flush, 73–74
  handle replacement, 77–78
  new, installing, 83–86
  old, removing, 81–82
  power-assisted flush, 74–75
Tools
  basic tools, 3, 5–7
  for bathroom clogs, 62–65
  buying tips, 11–12
  care and respect for, 14–15
  for carpentry, 9–10
  for electrical work, 9
  lending to others, 12–13
  for plumbing, 7–9
  renting, 13–14
  for tile work, 11
Torpedo levels, 7
Trap clogs, clearing, 64–65
Traps, drain system, 30

Trim, for laminate floor, 169–71
Tripped circuit breaker, 34, 36, 41–42
Trip-waste, tub shoe overflow, clearing, 70–71
Tubing cutters, 9, 28
Tub shoes
  clearing, 70–71
  functions of, 69
Twelve-gauge wire, 45
Two-wire NM 2G cable, 45

UF cable, 45
Undercounter lavatory, 87
Underground feed wire, 45

Venting system. *See* HVAC (heating, venting, air-conditioning) system
Vessel lavatory, 87
Voltage, circuit breaker box, 36

Wainscoting, 174–85
  baseboard/moldings, installing, 183–85
  beadboard, installing, 175–83
Wall-mounted lavatory, 87
Waste vent system, 30–31
Water damage
  walls, locating source, 159–60
  See also Basement, drying out

Water dispensers. *See* Refrigerator dispensers
Water service systems, 21–24
  potable/nonpotable water, 25
  private versus public, 22–24
  private wells/septic systems, 22
  public water/sewers, 21
  water meters, 24
Well pressure tank, 26
Well water, and septic systems, 22
Wires, electrical, types of, 45
Wire strippers, 9
Wrenches
  aluminum pipe types, 7
  basin cock, 7